Aboriginal Peoples in Urban Centres

Report of the National Round Table on Aboriginal Urban Issues

Royal Commission on Aboriginal Peoples

Available in Canada through
your local bookseller
or by mail from
Canada Communication Group – Publishing
Ottawa, Canada K1A 0S9

Canadian Cataloguing in Publication Data
National Round Table on Aboriginal Urban Issues
(1992: Edmonton, Alta.)
Aboriginal Peoples in urban centres: report of the
National Round Table on Aboriginal Urban Issues

Cat. no. Z1-1991/1-11-3E
ISBN 0-660-14964-8

1. Native peoples – Canada
2. Native peoples – Canada – Economic conditions
3. Native peoples – Canada – Social conditions
 I. Canada. Royal Commission on Aboriginal Peoples.
II. Title. III. Title: Report of the National Round Table on
Aboriginal Urban Issues.

E78.C2N37 1993   971'.00497   C93-099472-8

Also issued in French under the title:
Les peuples autochtones vivant en milieu urbain : rapport de la Table ronde nationale
sur les préoccupations des populations urbaines autochtones

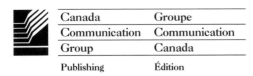

Canada	Groupe
Communication	Communication
Group	Canada
Publishing	Édition

Royal Commission
on Aboriginal Peoples

The following materials concerning the mandate and activities of the Royal Commission on Aboriginal Peoples have been prepared to assist members of the public with an interest in the Commission's work or in participating in the Commission's public consultation processes. The materials are available by writing to the Commission at the address below.

The Mandate, Royal Commission on Aboriginal Peoples, background documents
(August 1991)

The Right of Aboriginal Self-Government and the Constitution: A Commentary
(February 1992)

The Circle, RCAP newsletter

Terms of Reference, pamphlet

Speeches by Co-Chairs Dussault and Erasmus, Official launch of the public hearings, Winnipeg, 21 April 1992

"A Time to Talk - A Time to Listen", poster

Framing the Issues, Discussion paper no. 1
(October 1992)

Focusing the Dialogue, Discussion paper no. 2
(April 1993)

Focusing the Dialogue
(April 1993), video, available only to groups

Overview of the Second Round by Michael Cassidy
(April 1993)

Royal Commission on Aboriginal Peoples
P.O. Box 1993, Station B
Ottawa, Ontario K1P 1B2

Tel: (613) 943-2075 **Fax:** (613) 943-0304
Toll-free:
1-800-363-8235 (English, French, Chipewyan)
1-800-387-2148 (Cree, Inuktitut, Ojibwa)

Contents

Members of the
Royal Commission on
Aboriginal Peoples

René Dussault, j.c.a.
Co-Chair

Georges Erasmus
Co-Chair

Allan Blakeney
Commissioner

Paul Chartrand
Commissioner

Viola Marie Robinson
Commissioner

Mary Sillett
Commissioner

Bertha Wilson
Commissioner

Preface

The Royal Commission on Aboriginal Peoples has undertaken to host a series of National Round Tables on selected themes. The Round Tables bring together academics, practitioners, political leaders and community leaders with knowledge and expertise on the selected themes in order to assist the Commission in the preparation of recommendations for the final report.

The National Round Tables all have a similar format. We invite certain experts or leading-edge thinkers to produce papers on a series of questions that we intend to ask participants to consider. In the course of panel presentations, round table discussions and plenary sessions, participants have the opportunity to put forward their views and recommendations as they relate to the questions.

The published proceedings of the National Round Tables will help to inform the general public about the issues addressed there. It is anticipated that publication of the round table proceedings will prompt further consideration of the ideas and debate captured in the reports and encourage Canadians to come forward at the public hearings or to make written submissions with further thoughts and recommendations.

We are deeply indebted to all participants in the National Round Table on Aboriginal Urban Issues for their input and advice, and to Dan David, who wrote the issues papers and the report on the round table workshops.

This report of the proceedings is intended to stimulate further dialogue and positive changes in policy. Your views and recommendations on this important issue are welcome. We invite you to write to us at the address set out elsewhere in this document and to appear before us when we hold public hearings in your area.

René Dussault, j.c.a.
Co-Chair

Georges Erasmus
Co-Chair

Commission
Report

From June 21 to 23, 1992, the Royal Commission on Aboriginal Peoples hosted a national round table on urban Aboriginal issues. The event, held in Edmonton, Alberta, brought together a wide range of individuals from nine Canadian cities with significant Aboriginal populations: Vancouver, Edmonton, Calgary, Regina, Saskatoon, Winnipeg, Toronto, Montreal and Halifax. Of the 200 participants, both Aboriginal and non-Aboriginal, a majority came from the urban Aboriginal community and many of them are involved in social services delivery.

National round tables on issues of broad public concern form part of the Commission's continuing public consultation process. The round table on urban issues was organized around four themes, focusing on services, governance, economics, and health and wellness. The conference consisted of sixteen concurrent workshops on the four theme areas, as well as plenary sessions for all participants. An overview of the workshop proceedings, prepared for the Commission, is presented later in this volume.

A large and growing proportion of Aboriginal people live in urban centres, and the realities of their lives were brought home to the Commission not only at the round table but also in public hearings, held during 1992 in larger cities such as Winnipeg, Toronto, and Halifax and in smaller ones such as Thunder Bay and Yellowknife. Urban Aboriginal issues will also be a focus of research carried out in 1993 under the sponsorship of the Commission.

At both the round table and the public hearings, the Commission heard moving accounts of the issues that regularly confront Aboriginal people living in urban settings. The central themes that emerged are as follows:

- the survival of Aboriginal identity in an environment that is usually indifferent and often hostile to Aboriginal cultures;
- the existing void in government policies to recognize and reinforce the goals of urban Aboriginal people;
- the need for accessible and appropriate human services; and
- difficult questions around how urban Aboriginal people can gain an effective voice in governance and decision making.

The purpose of this report is to focus public attention on urban Aboriginal issues and to encourage broad participation, by Aboriginal and non-Aboriginal people, civic leaders, and policy makers, in seeking answers to the questions raised at the round table and in other consultations carried out by the Commission.

Urban Aboriginal People: Who Are They?

From the territories and northern regions of the provinces, from the east coast and the west coast, they migrate to the cities from Métis settlements, Indian reserves and Inuit communities, from many nations and diverse lifestyles. Some are born in the city, others choose to locate there, seeking a better life for themselves and their children. Still others end up in cities, unable or unwilling to find their way back to their home communities after release from prison, TB hospital or foster care.

Over the past thirty years the Aboriginal population in Canada has become increasingly urbanized. Pushed from their home communities by poor economic conditions, substandard housing, limited educational opportunities, and social problems – and pulled to urban centres by the potential for education, employment and health care – increasing numbers of Aboriginal people are taking up urban life. Speaking at the round table, Winston McKay painted this common scene:

> Last week, thinking about this meeting, I sat down with my son-in-law and we named about 200 families who had left our Métis village of Cumberland House in the last few years. Some are in the towns where our people traditionally went to find work: Flin Flon, Thompson, The Pas. Some are in Winnipeg and as far away as British Columbia. Some have been pulled to the cities by opportunities for work or education or a more comfortable life. But most of them have been pushed out of the home community because life there was no longer good.

Aboriginal people who find steady employment and social acceptance in the city blend into the increasingly multicultural city scene, while those who encounter difficulties retain high visibility and reinforce the stereotype of urban Aboriginal people as poor, marginal and problem-ridden. Some Aboriginal urban residents are transient, moving back and forth between the city and their home communities. Many others stay permanently in urban areas or are second- or third-generation urban dwellers.

Presentations to the Commission indicated that whether they live in cities for a short time or plan to stay there permanently, Aboriginal people in urban centres often face overwhelming problems that are rooted in cultural dislocation and powerlessness, discrimination and economic hardship. In workshops and plenary sessions at the round table and in hearings across the country, they spoke of their experiences, the importance of their identity, their frustrations with governments and service agencies, and their determination to exercise influence over the institutions that govern their daily lives.

Indian, Inuit and Métis Identities

One speaker on urban issues declared, "We don't leave our identity at the edge of the city." Crossing the city limits does not transform Aboriginal people into non-Aboriginal people; they go on being the particular kind of person they have always been – Cree, Dene, Mohawk, Haida. The intention of Aboriginal people to go on being here, to go on expressing their Aboriginal identity and to pass it on to their children, was a consistent theme in presentations by urban Aboriginal people at the round table and in hearings across the country.

Elders are concerned that as Aboriginal languages are lost, the understanding of where Aboriginal people come from, their connection to the land, the awareness that all life is related and interdependent, will also be lost. Adults who remember their traditions wrestle with the problem of how to sustain physical, emotional, mental and spiritual balance in an environment where relationships are fragmented and impersonal and meeting their families' basic needs is a daily struggle. Young people growing up in the city ask, "Where can I go to learn who I am? Where are the elders who can teach me? How should I approach them?" The homeless, the alienated, the street children were seldom present in person at Commission hearings, but their presence was felt in the stories of neglect, exploitation and untimely death told by workers and kin whose mission it is to restore health to all their relations.

Some urban Aboriginal people sustain their identity through contacts with their places of origin or with elders they have sought out as teachers. Others have been away so long that they have lost touch with relatives. Still others, who have been forced from their homes and communities as a result of intermarriage or domestic violence, keep their distance out of fear of rejection or further violence.

The diversity of origins and cultures of Aboriginal people living in a particular city often poses difficulties in establishing a sense of community, even for those whose ties with their homelands and original communities have weakened over time. Differences in Aboriginal status and entitlements may also interfere with collective efforts to address shared concerns.

Individuals often identify with their nation: Métis, Dakota, Micmac. They may have gained or regained status under the Bill C-31 amendments to the *Indian Act*, which removed much of the legal discrimination against women who married non-Indians; in practice, however, the law failed in many cases to provide a genuine opportunity to take up residence on already overcrowded reserves. They may be members of nations that signed treaties in return for rights that they, as urban residents living off-reserve, have been unable in practice to assert. They may be Métis, whose unique status as a nation born from the joining of two peoples and cultures has been ignored and devalued historically and who have been deprived of homelands through government neglect and the sharp practices of land speculators. With increasing frequency, they are Inuit who have been drawn to the city by prospects of education and jobs, or who have failed to find their way home after periods spent in southern hospitals or prisons.

Whatever their local and cultural origins, Aboriginal people living in urban centres share with reserve-based, rural and northern Aboriginal people the struggle to gain recognition as First Peoples, members of Canadian society who have a human right and, it can be argued, a constitutional right to survive as peoples, wherever in this land they choose to live.

The Policy Vacuum

Whatever other rights pursuant to treaty or otherwise that Aboriginal people might have, they have the same rights and are entitled to the same services as are available to all other urban dwellers. One presenter at the round table pointed out that if he wanted to merge into the general population, institutions are already there to be used. However, if his goal is to retain or regain his Indian-ness there does not seem to be a vehicle.

Section 91.24 of the *Constitution Act, 1867* assigns legislative authority to Parliament for "Indians, and Lands reserved for the Indians". This power has been exercised principally through the *Indian Act*, first enacted in 1876 and amended most recently in 1985. Although the federal government has exclusive power to legislate with respect to Indians (and Inuit, according to a 1939 Supreme Court interpretation of section 91.24), provincial and municipal governments have often introduced programs that respond to the distinctive needs of citizens, as they have done, for example, with respect to immigrants.

The federal government has generally restricted its provision of services to Indians living on reserves and to Inuit and Indians living in northern communities. With the exception of some education and health benefits, federal services are not available once Indians leave a reserve or Inuit and Indians leave their northern communities. Métis and all others who are not Indians as defined by the *Indian Act* receive no services under federal legislation.

Like Canadians generally, Aboriginal people living in cities look to provincial and municipal governments for public services. In recent years some provincial governments have introduced special programs of limited scope – often in the form of pilot projects – but for the most part provincial governments continue to treat Aboriginal people in urban centres as part of the general population. Municipalities derive a major part of their funding from provincial grants and therefore limit services to those mandated and subsidized by the province. Thus, for example, classes in English or French as a second language may be available to the children of immigrants but, despite similar needs, few such programs exist for Aboriginal children entering school without an adequate knowledge of English or French.

Presenters at the round table reported frequently that applications for services result in their being shuffled from one level of government to another and served by none. Lobbying to upgrade provincial services for Aboriginal people often meets the response that the federal government is trying to off-load its responsibilities to the provinces.

Members of nations that signed treaties are particularly critical of the restrictions on their treaty entitlements when they leave their reserves. They argue that their treaty rights are portable and should be available to individuals regardless of their place of residence. Eric Robinson, of the Aboriginal Council of Winnipeg, told the Commission in Winnipeg:

> The Department of Indian Affairs has said repeatedly that they do not service any Treaty Indians outside the boundaries of their reserves. We'd like to say that this is wrong and we continue to say that our treaty rights are portable and services should be provided, even in urban centres like Winnipeg. Our people...have become disillusioned, often being treated as third- or fourth-class citizens.

Non-Aboriginal organizations that try to extend support are also limited by restrictions imposed by government policies. In Toronto, the Commission heard from Dan Haggerty of the Canadian Executive Service Organization (CESO), a non-profit, non-governmental body that provides volunteer consultants for the development and management of Aboriginal businesses and communities in Canada:

> The CESO Native Program receives most of its funding from the Department of Indian Affairs and Northern Development and, as can be expected, this is earmarked exclusively for work with status Indians and Inuit. Therefore, CESO has not been able to extend routinely its services to Métis and off-reserve Indians, except in Alberta where some provincial funding is available for Métis people. Services to urban Aboriginal people have also suffered from these constraints. It has become very difficult for CESO to provide services to Friendship Centres and other Aboriginal urban organizations.

Aboriginal governments and organizations, operating within the limits of federal and provincial program funding, are powerless to fill the policy vacuum. Umbrella organizations such as the Urban Representative Body of Aboriginal Nations (URBAN) in Vancouver have been developed, but they lack the tax base and legislative authority to compensate for the lack of policy and programs emanating from all levels of government. Such organizations must incorporate as non-profit societies under provincial legislation and compete with other voluntary groups for discretionary program funding – often without success if the culturally based program needs of urban Aboriginal people are not recognized as legitimate and Aboriginal organizations are thought to be duplicating existing services.

Inappropriate and Inadequate Services

The policy vacuum, which is not being filled effectively by any level of government, results inevitably in serious deficiencies in public services for Aboriginal people in urban centres. The first problem with services relates to the fundamental nature of needs; the second relates to the structure and financing of services to respond to the needs.

In Commission hearings, Aboriginal people stated repeatedly that they want holistic services that recognize and work to heal the effects of the wrongs they have suffered. They say that the poverty of Aboriginal people is related to dispossession from lands and resources and the persistent failure of public education. They say that alcohol addiction and family breakdown are related to the oppression and abuses of the residential school experience. They say that low self-esteem, which leads to carelessness about life and health, is reinforced by racism encountered daily with employers, landlords, schoolmates. They say that they need spiritual renewal and restoration of culture in order to become whole human beings again.

Especially in urban centres, where Aboriginal people must turn to agencies set up for the general population, social services tend to be directed toward dealing with specific problems, such as unemployment, child neglect or suicide; they therefore address symptoms in isolation rather than helping to restore wholeness to an injured people. Many Aboriginal people maintain that because present ills have resulted from the misuse of power by public authorities, Aboriginal people – whether living in cities or on reserves – have a legitimate claim to culturally appropriate services that promote healing through a holistic approach to individuals and communities. They also argue that services should be adapted to their lifeways, not determined by the bureaucratic divisions that undermine the effectiveness of existing social services.

Aboriginal people speaking at the round table and public hearings said that parallel services staffed by Aboriginal people are the most effective means of responding to the needs they identified. They spoke of the lack of services for people with disabilities, for Aboriginal people with AIDS, for street youth and for elders. Métis Senator Thelma Chalifoux told the Commission in Winnipeg:

> There are no homes for our Métis seniors or Indian seniors living off-reserve. There are no services for them. They are totally isolated because the existing services do not have Aboriginal people that could look in on them and counsel them. Our veterans are in the same boat. I visit veterans that live in one little shack, one little room, and they have nothing, and they're too proud to ask.

In cities across Canada there are now housing projects, child care agencies, education and training institutions, and street patrols staffed and administered by Aboriginal people. Still the resources are inadequate to satisfy the depth of need. The agencies are often staffed by underpaid Aboriginal employees supplemented by volunteer labour. Cultural or experiential qualifications of their personnel are not recognized by funding agencies. Innovations in service design are frustrated by limitations imposed by federal or provincial regulations or funding restrictions. Aboriginal agencies must compete for funding with non-Aboriginal institutions.

The solution frequently proposed to provide institutional stability to Aboriginal service agencies is to recognize Aboriginal authority in the areas of funding and programming. Earl Magnusson, Director of Urban Development for the

Federation of Saskatchewan Indian Nations, told the Commission at Wahpeton, Saskatchewan:

> To properly address and implement the needed services and program-ming, resources must be channelled directly to Indian control in urban centres. Without the actual transfer of financial and program-ming authorities to accountable, Indian-controlled groups, the status quo will remain.

Although participants at the round table universally supported Aboriginal involvement in the design and delivery of services, there was debate over the form that involvement should take. Some Aboriginal people argue that cultural differences should be reflected in service delivery, to protect separate identities and rights. Yvon Dumont, speaking for the Métis National Council at the launch of hearings in Winnipeg, said:

> At this moment we're looking at strictly Métis institutions for Métis people. We feel that by agreeing to be lumped in with all other Aboriginal people we run the chance of losing our identity as an Aboriginal people. So we feel that it is important that we concentrate right now on developing and protecting Métis culture and heritage.

Other Aboriginal people believe that the common challenges faced by urban residents demand a unified approach. They advocate 'status-blind' institutions to deliver services to Aboriginal people, regardless of their cultural identity or legal status. Della Maquire said in Halifax:

> The way I see Native issues, we're all suffering from the same types of abuse, even though there are cultural and language differences....We should relate to each other and help each other, treat everyone equally.

Urban Aboriginal Government

In the summer of 1992, Aboriginal, federal, provincial and territorial leaders reached consensus on recognizing the inherent right of self-government for Aboriginal peoples within Canada, including those living off-reserve and in urban centres. Although the Charlottetown Accord failed to receive approval in a national referendum held on October 26, 1992, Aboriginal people have stated that they will continue to pursue implementation of the rights recognized in the Accord even without a constitutional amendment.

The form that urban Aboriginal government might take is subject to debate. Some urban Aboriginal people advocate the retention of political linkages with bands, province-wide federations, treaty organizations, or land-based governments. Other urban Aboriginal people argue that their interests have not been well served by land-based governments or existing Aboriginal political organizations. As a consequence, they support the development of separate bodies to represent their interests. Organizations such as URBAN in Vancouver, the Native Canadian Centre in Toronto, and the Aboriginal Council of Winnipeg, which originated as agencies or councils of agencies serving social and cultural needs, are considered by some as a natural base for new functions, providing a vehicle for political action emerging specifically from the urban Aboriginal community.

Presentations at the round table and in public hearings made it clear that no single form of urban Aboriginal government is likely to be appropriate for every city in Canada, given the diversity of communities and populations. Workable models and approaches adopted in centres across the country will need to reflect the diverse circumstances, characteristics and choices of the communities in question. Regardless of the form they prefer, however, urban Aboriginal people are unanimous in asserting that they must have a voice in the decisions that affect their daily lives. In the future, that voice may take several diverse forms within existing municipal councils and school boards or through autonomous urban institutions mandated to provide services or to exercise a range of government functions. It may also be heard through institutions of urban governance that are extensions of current Aboriginal political structures. Whatever arrangements develop, however, the criteria for their establishment and acceptance have been made clear in testimony before the Commission: responsibility, accountability, and responsiveness to the urban Aboriginal constituencies they serve.

A Call to Action

The Commission's analysis of presentations made at the round table and in public hearings in 1992 raises fundamental questions that demand a response:

- Do non-Aboriginal Canadians agree that Aboriginal people living in urban centres have the right to preserve and promote their distinct cultures, identities and languages? If so, how can individual non-Aboriginal citizens and their governments and institutions help Aboriginal people to make their right a reality?

- How will policies that recognize the needs of urban Aboriginal people be developed? What role will urban Aboriginal people play in the development of such policies? What government has responsibility for filling the vacuum that now exists? By what means will urban Aboriginal people ensure that the vacuum is filled?

- In what geographic and service areas are parallel Aboriginal service agencies necessary or desirable? How will the issue of 'status-blind' or distinct Indian, Métis and Inuit services be resolved? What authorities and funding processes are required to provide stability to parallel agencies? Where Aboriginal services continue to be delivered by non-Aboriginal institutions, how can they be adapted to serve urban Aboriginal people more effectively?
- How will the inherent right of Aboriginal peoples to self-government be implemented in urban centres? Under what authority? In what forms? With what powers? What constituencies will be represented in urban Aboriginal governments? How will urban Aboriginal governments relate to federal, provincial and municipal governments?

The Commission will be addressing these and other questions in collaboration with Aboriginal communities and federal, provincial, territorial and municipal governments, in research projects and hearings during 1993. The results of these efforts will contribute to the formulation of the Commission's recommendations in our final report. We invite Aboriginal and non-Aboriginal people to participate in the deliberations of the Commission so that recommendations on these issues reflect the broadest possible consensus on what is needed and what can be achieved.

Action on the pressing human concerns conveyed to the Commission and touched upon in this document cannot and should not await our report. We cannot turn a blind eye to the evils of extreme poverty, homelessness, substance abuse, suicide and racism. The exploitation of Aboriginal children on the streets of Canadian cities cannot be allowed to continue. The neglect of elders who are too isolated or too proud to seek out services cannot be tolerated. Canada must recognize, indeed celebrate, the presence of Aboriginal peoples in our society and accord them their rightful place as Canada's first peoples.

We urge municipal leaders, school boards, police forces, social services providers, and provincial and federal governments to join forces now with urban Aboriginal people to address the issues set out in this report and to assist the Commission in formulating long-range solutions. The time for action is long overdue. The consequence of inaction can only be deepening crisis, as Aboriginal people continue to respond in increasing numbers to the pushes and pulls that propel them into urban centres across the country.

Report on
the Workshops

*Dan David**

There are more Aboriginal people living in urban centres across Canada than there are living in Aboriginal territories and communities – on reserves, in Métis settlements and in Inuit communities. Despite the growing number of Aboriginal urban people and the increasing realization that they constitute a permanent presence in urban centres across Canada, little attention has been paid to them and their needs by either land-based Aboriginal governments, Aboriginal organizations or non-Aboriginal governments. They and their problems remain largely invisible in Canada's cities.

"The indigenous self-help groups," noted Lloyd Barber, former president of the University of Regina, "are either not sufficiently funded, not sufficiently encouraged, or are looked upon either askance or with outright suspicion and negative attitudes so that the situation tends to complicate itself and tends to evolve negatively instead of positively."

The migration by Aboriginal people into urban centres continues as a result of many of the same pressures that provoked the initial migration in the 1960s. "The flow of First Nations people to and from urban areas is not going to decrease, as we heard last night," Michael Thrasher, a cross-cultural consultant, warned delegates attending the round table on urban issues in Edmonton. "It's going to increase."

* Prepared for the Royal Commission on Aboriginal Peoples by Dan David, Handsome Lake Productions. Opinions expressed in this report are those of Mr. David and do not necessarily reflect the opinion or position of the Commission.

"When it comes to urban questions," explained Lloyd Barber, "there is no single unifying band or national status for status Indians in urban areas. It is also further complicated by Bill C-31 (1985 Amendment to the *Indian Act*) people. It's a complicating if not divisive issue.... You have the non-status people who have no band or First Nation or at least who have had none for long enough that they have no affinity with any particular band."

"They have an Aboriginal affinity, an Aboriginal affiliation, but no home base to which they can readily refer. And then, at least on the prairies, the distinct and particular situation of Métis people who not only see themselves as a distinct and separate group but are."

These internal divisions and cultural distinctions are a hallmark of Aboriginal urban life. This has led to the beginning of a new life experience – the Aboriginal urban experience. At the same time, however, the constant mix of transient and stable Aboriginal urban populations has created unique problems and situations that demand uniquely Aboriginal urban solutions.

It was hoped that this National Round Table on Aboriginal Urban Issues would foster a dialogue to advance these solutions. The round table was structured as a series of small workshops so that each participant could contribute to the discussion. The source material for this report was notes taken at the workshops by INFOLINK Consultants. These notes were augmented by the author's personal notes and audio recordings.

With respect to style and language, many of the delegates used the term Indian or Métis when referring to themselves or their group. Some used the term Native in the context of expressions such as in 'Native spirituality'. Mostly, they used the term Native when speaking about Aboriginal peoples, which includes all Indian, Inuit and Métis peoples. Where the delegates have been quoted directly, the word 'Native' has been retained. In some cases, the term is part of the title of an organization or service, for instance, Native Council of Canada. These references have also been retained.

The conclusions and interpretations in this report are those of the author and may not reflect the views of the Royal Commission on Aboriginal Peoples. The author is solely responsible for the accuracy of material in this report.

Services

General Statements

Participants in service workshops had been asked to arrange their topics in order of importance and to pick one topic that was more important than the others. Participants said, however, that this was impossible. Whether it was services for people with disabilities, education or housing, they said each topic was equally important and deserved equal attention. Other group members said service delivery issues are symptoms of deeper problems of governance, racism, powerlessness and cultural breakdown that must be resolved.

Participants identified several key service delivery areas which, they emphasized, are linked. Education, for instance, was tied to AIDS, disabilities and health. Addictions, participants said, had much to do with cultural awareness, poverty and joblessness. Some participants from different cities reported different key areas of concern, but they said this may have had as much to do with the availability of government funding as it had with problems in their regions. Some of the key service areas they outlined were as follows:

- education
- addictions
- disability
- AIDS
- homelessness
- child care
- social services
- health
- housing
- cultural awareness/isolation
- employment
- transportation

This was by no means a complete list of issues or concerns. Many of the delegates spoke at length about the divisions within Aboriginal urban communities and of the frustrations of constantly chasing program dollars, of providing essential services with dwindling resources, and of their over-reliance on the aid of volunteers.

Some delegates reported problems that are specific to an area or region of the country. Perhaps nowhere was this more evident than in the comments of delegates from Quebec, who mentioned racist attitudes, uncertainty about the political future, and the problems of distance and cultural and linguistic isolation.

> Language is a huge problem for Aboriginal people in Quebec. It's not only the French/English problem, but the fact that many Aboriginal people have lost their Aboriginal language.

The delegates identified friendship centres as the primary vehicle of service delivery to Aboriginal people in urban centres. Friendship centres were described as "the point of first contact" that many Aboriginal people have with an urban social service agency. In some cases, other Aboriginal urban service agencies had grown out of programs first developed by friendship centres. In other cases, friendship centres continue to be the sole delivery mechanisms for a particular service.

Friendship centres were praised for the services they provide to Aboriginal urban people. So too were other urban-based Aboriginal services such as court workers programs, Aboriginal interpreter programs in hospitals and courts, and Aboriginal women's shelters.

Despite the efforts of Aboriginal institutions like friendship centres, the majority of the workshop participants agreed that services for Aboriginal urban people are generally inadequate.

Inadequate Services

Participants said Aboriginal people are moving to the cities in increasing numbers. They described people who find a bewildering and confusing city, with strange ways and laws. One participant said some Aboriginal people arrive unaware of modern conveniences.

> Some of these people who come into the city don't know how to turn the tap or turn on electrical appliances – even getting on the elevator.

Many Aboriginal people have difficulty finding the services they need. They are unfamiliar with the city, its institutions and how these agencies work. The faces are unfamiliar; language, customs and manners are strange. The participants said a first visit to a non-Aboriginal agency could be an intimidating experience for an Aboriginal person.

The participants said non-Aboriginal agencies have different goals and priorities from Aboriginal social service agencies. Aboriginal agencies, such as friendship centres, view an individual person's problems as "symptoms of deeper problems" that are rooted in "racism, powerlessness and cultural breakdown". The non-Aboriginal agencies, they said, tended to look at conditions as isolated problems and to view the individual as deficient. As a result, the workshop participants said, Aboriginal agencies are trusted more than non-Aboriginal agencies by Aboriginal urban people.

> Social service workers outside Aboriginal service organizations lack cross-cultural training and are ignorant of the special problems faced by Aboriginal urban people.

The participants said this lack of cross-cultural understanding has led to some traumatic consequences for Aboriginal urban families. For instance, the participants said many Aboriginal women are wary of reporting sexual abuse or refuse to enter substance abuse programs for fear that non-Aboriginal child welfare agencies will take their children away and place them in foster care.

> Culturally appropriate counselling and care facilities with trained staff are required to deal with child abuse and incest. It won't work to place survivors in a non-Aboriginal environment. The whole family needs training, not just the victim. Aboriginal counsellors should be trained, and Aboriginal communities must take over control of child and family services.

The participants said the lack of appropriate Aboriginal services compels many Aboriginal people to avoid seeking help or treatment. This only makes matters worse.

> Health problems are magnified when there is no liaison for Aboriginal people using the medical system, no transportation, or when they don't seek prenatal care.

Participants said there are too few Aboriginal urban programs. They are understaffed, underfunded and too dependent upon unpaid, untrained volunteers. They said burnout of volunteers and staff is a real danger. The numbers of people seeking help and the severity of the problems are increasing. Despite these conditions, the participants said they face more cutbacks in funding.

> The possibility of cutbacks in program funding has impaired the effectiveness of front-line staff and has made long-term planning virtually impossible.

As a result, workshop participants said, the level and quality of service are degenerating. Services have always been inadequate to deal with the problems of the Aboriginal urban population but they are getting worse because of cutbacks. This leaves many staff working "full-time on the survival" of their programs and this means less time for everyone to meet the needs of the client.

Still, the participants said, in some cases, there are simply no services available because programs are non-existent.

Lack of Services

Participants emphasized the need for Aboriginal services that are designed, staffed and run by Aboriginal people to reach those who need help in the Aboriginal urban community. In some cases, however, these services simply do not exist.

People with disabilities

Participants pointed out that there are no services available for Aboriginal people with disabilities who move from reserves to urban settings.

Street youth

A large number of street youth are involved in prostitution, participants said, and there are no services waiting for them when they are ready to leave the street. There are long waiting lists for support programs and no group homes under Aboriginal control.

Child welfare

Participants deplored the lack of program support for Aboriginal children who have been adopted into non-Aboriginal families, stripped of their cultural identity, and forced to be 'white'.

AIDS

A special hospice is needed for Aboriginal people who are HIV-positive, participants said. An Aboriginal liaison between agencies is needed here as well. We need people to do more than just laundry, said a participant; we need emotional counselling and support as well. Culture is also important. A hospice needs to be staffed and run by Aboriginal people, participants argued, not just culturally sensitive people.

Participants condemned the absence of appropriate services for Aboriginal urban people in these cases. They pointed to women who have been 'blackballed' in their home communities for pressing charges or even raising the issue of family abuse, sexual abuse and child abuse. They may be victims themselves. Yet, upon arriving in the city, there are few shelters, support services or counselling.

Many Aboriginal people are referred routinely to non-Aboriginal services where they are subjected to discrimination. Their cases may not be deemed "serious enough" for emergency service; the attitude expressed may be that such situations are "normal" in Aboriginal communities.

This attitude, the participants admitted, extends to Aboriginal service agencies as well. They hear the plea for help but they feel overwhelmed by their caseloads and the enormity of the social problems they have to deal with daily. One participant said:

> The message needs to get out that 'emergency' means just that. I recently saw a notice advising clients to make appointments three weeks in advance. A person with an emergency need could hardly wait for three weeks! 'Emergency' means now!

Funding

Participants said their programs all endure a chronic lack of funding. As a result, they cannot provide the level of service, the types of services and the length of support that people need. For instance, one participant said, governments insist that timeframes be set for the length of support and counselling that people receive. The service agencies, including Aboriginal agencies, acquiesce to these constraints to the detriment of the clients.

> Communities need to recognize both the need for family counselling and how the counselling process works. There is treatment lasting three to six months and after-care for two to three years. To put it simply, extend service hours. Currently, we operate on 30 hours of counselling per client and it's falling short.

However, as participants pointed out, many of the funding problems are the result of a jurisdictional void that exists for Aboriginal people in urban areas.

> Most of us are always fighting for dollars, to keep our administration going, to house ourselves, and look after our administration costs, whether we're Métis, Treaty, whatever. And we felt if we could all be in one building then those dollars we're all fighting over could be better used to service our clients. Because we give people the runaround now when they come into the city. Well, you're Treaty and you've not been here one year so you go to this place. But, oh no, you've been here a year already so you go to this place. Well, you're Métis, you have to go somewhere else. It's too confusing for people.

Participants argued that services to Aboriginal urban people could not be based on legal definitions imposed by non-Aboriginal governments. Many said services should be "status-blind" to ensure, for instance, that Aboriginal literacy programs would be offered to all Aboriginal people regardless of their status. The Aboriginal urban population is too transient, varied and diverse to make separate services practical. This, however, means redefining jurisdictions and mandates.

Jurisdiction

Many people said that jurisdictional issues are the number one problem for Aboriginal urban people. In most cases, the federal government refers status Indians back to their bands for services but it is inconsistent in providing services to the off-reserve population. It funds some programs but not others. Participants pointed to similar actions by provincial governments, which some participants said impose jurisdiction over areas such as education, but then deny responsibility when it comes time to pay for the services.

The result is that some Aboriginal people can be served by Aboriginal services while others are not. Participants agreed that jurisdictional problems hinder their social and political development in urban centres and prevented them from co-ordinating services to Aboriginal urban people.

Disregarding the position of non-Aboriginal governments on jurisdictional matters, participants concentrated on the political positions of Aboriginal political organizations. Participants recognize that such questions have not been addressed by the Aboriginal organizations. There is just as much of a jurisdictional void within Aboriginal political organizations as within non-Aboriginal governments.

> I don't know about other cities, but in Winnipeg there's a real divide on who should be in control of what. So how do you work with the idea that status people want control of all resources earmarked for status. Métis people want control of resources earmarked for Métis people. And how do you bring that together in an urban setting where, as service providers, we have to provide services status-blind.

Some participants referred to innovative programs such as the Anishnawbe Health Centre in Toronto and friendship centres that provided status-blind services to Aboriginal urban people. These institutions were hailed as examples where "the need to provide help" to Aboriginal urban people overrides political considerations and positions. However, participants noted that these programs are limited in scope, and many services are not included in their mandates because of jurisdictional difficulties.

"What about education?" one participant asked. Another wondered about abuse counselling or mental health. Many of the participants said they need new urban structures to represent the unique situation of Aboriginal urban people on a status-blind basis.

The president of the National Association of Friendship Centres said there was a need for Aboriginal urban people to redefine their identities in terms of their urban situations. Whatever model they decided upon, he said, it had to be both accountable to and representative of all Aboriginal urban people and not just certain groups.

> The situation now before us is a process used for centuries to divide and conquer, and we're grabbing at it. We're the biggest industry in this country. Everyone is claiming to speak on behalf of a group, but the urban people are saying that's not correct: there's nobody there to help us... We want to resolve this issue, we need to resolve this issue, because if we don't, we're the ones who will suffer.

Other participants insisted their identity is tied to their homelands. They said their cultural identities as First Nations people are tied to their communities, just as the identities of Métis flow from their settlements. The answer was for each group to extend jurisdiction from these home territories over the Aboriginal urban population. Several others disagreed.

> You know, that's okay if you live in the community, but what about if you're in the city? Who represents us in the city? You talk about self-government; fine, we get organized in the city. We're going to move ahead and we can grow as a community. I really believe this because we're doing it in Montreal. But what if you don't trust your governments back home in the community?

The discussion reached an impasse. Participants agreed there had be some way of co-ordinating the delivery of services to Aboriginal urban people. They agreed there should be 'centres of service' where these services could be concentrated. However, participants could not reach consensus on the political structure to administer a "local urban government" of this type.

Not everyone was happy with the discussion.

The director of an Aboriginal urban youth organization in Vancouver said her clientele is composed mainly of street kids, whose lives in the city are marked by prostitution, pimping, drug dealing, and addiction. In the downtown east side of Vancouver, 60 per cent of social service clients are of Aboriginal origin, and 40 per cent of those are street youth. She said it was frustrating that the round table had focused mainly on jurisdiction.

> It's hard for me to really put a lot of effort into trying to solve that problem when I see 14- and 15-year-old kids dying on a daily basis, as a result of crime, overdoses, and HIV/AIDS. I don't really give a damn about the legal issues. I just want to make sure our kids are going to live.

Education

The Royal Commission asked round table participants to consider these questions:

> Who should run schools? Should there be separate schools? The Commission is looking at what urban structure is needed; one agency for all, or separate institutions?

Participants said that "education is the single most important issue facing Aboriginal people." They told the Royal Commission that the education system, as it exists, is failing Aboriginal urban people.

Participants said they expect the education system to do more than teach their children how to read and write. What children are taught has much to do with forming society's attitudes about Aboriginal people and affects the Aboriginal student's self-esteem and self-worth.

> Public education is needed to effect changes in attitudes about Aboriginal people. The media only comes out when something negative happens, it doesn't cover positive events. There is a real lack of awareness about Aboriginal people and their issues.

> The attitudes of non-Aboriginal students discourage some Aboriginal students from returning to school.

Participants said the problem begins with the materials used in schools. They said that teaching materials in western Canada are "strongly biased against Aboriginal people." The materials do not include or reflect their history and perceptions or explain current Aboriginal issues.

> The education system does not reflect Aboriginal values or traditions and fails to address the crisis issues facing Aboriginal communities. Outdated, culturally inappropriate teaching models are still in use.

As a result of the poor image of Aboriginal people transmitted through course materials:

> School has a negative connotation for many Aboriginal children. It's very easy for them to drop out.

The participants said attempts to change the course materials, by developing more appropriate school books for instance, had met with mixed results. Some provincial education ministries have considered such proposals. However, the participants said:

> Provinces have total control of education policy, but there is a need for 'consumers' of education services to be heard. Some provincial departments of education have come to the conclusion that it is less expensive to buy textbooks in bulk than to support the development of local curriculum resources. In Alberta, an effort to build an Aboriginal component into the history program was shelved in the 1970s, due to a lack of funding.

Participants said territorial or reserve-based programs, developed by Aboriginal people, have resulted in changes to some course materials in these communities but there had been little change in the course materials used by urban school boards.

However, participants said there is a problem caused by having two systems of education – one federal, for reserves, and another provincial, in urban areas. The standards are sometimes different and so are the courses.

Indian students coming out of federal schools have not been taught according to approved provincial curriculum. The problem should be addressed by developing a comprehensive education plan for urban centres.

The participants suggested that Aboriginal urban people run their own schools and where population warrants, perhaps even set up their own school boards. Aboriginal education programs have been developed specifically for the Aboriginal population in urban centres. However, the participants said the curriculum, course content and the method of evaluation vary from school board to school board, from city to city, and from province to province.

> The quality of Aboriginal education programs tends to vary from one community to another. In Edmonton, a community-based program serves Aboriginal students in a number of different schools. In Manitoba, by contrast, there is no comprehensive curriculum, history is not compulsory, and students' learning is very fragmented.

According to the participants, special Aboriginal education programs are often viewed as substandard by non-Aboriginal educators and administrators.

> Many Native schools in urban areas face negative perceptions, despite high academic standards in some programs.

However, these Aboriginal programs reflect an awareness of the special rights of Aboriginal people, such as treaty rights, while non-Aboriginal programs sometimes do not. Thus, students in Aboriginal programs are more likely to be properly advised with respect to any benefits or aid to which they might be entitled.

Even so, participants said that these entitlements or services are often under-funded. As a result, some students cannot afford to pursue their education.

> There is often a waiting list for funded services. Students with treaty rights are often unable to obtain the services to which they are entitled.

Many of the problems, participants said, might be addressed by allowing Aboriginal parents a say in how their children are educated.

> A solution to this problem could be alternative Aboriginal education within the regular school system. There could be an Aboriginal advisory committee to direct the school board on Aboriginal cultural issues. The schools will require extra funds for Aboriginal students.

Some participants felt programs like this should be integrated by school boards across the country in urban centres. The courses developed through programs such as these would be included in the general curriculum and not be confined only to Aboriginal students.

> Indian and Métis studies should be part of the overall high school curriculum, not just for Aboriginal students.

> Aboriginal studies is an option in many school systems, but some participants felt it should be compulsory for any student who wishes to complete high school. Denying Aboriginal history means denying the heritage of students who are attending Canadian schools.

For some Métis participants, this proposal was viewed as preferable to some other proposals for several reasons. They felt that while First Nations people could have a choice of school systems— the federal or the provincial – Métis had no choice but with the provincial system and civic school boards.

> It is particularly important for Métis people that the public school system change, since Métis are not likely to leave the system.

Participants considered how to ensure greater Aboriginal representation on school boards. A delegate from Saskatchewan noted that the presence of a lone Aboriginal person on the Regina school board had not brought down that city's high dropout rate, although it was noted that the lone Aboriginal member has had a "huge impact" in her first year of office. In Winnipeg, there is talk of forming an Aboriginal school board consisting of the fourteen schools with large Aboriginal populations.

The participants wondered how much real control over their children's education these suggestions would give Aboriginal parents in urban centres. They noted that

> ...education funds for reserves come from Indian Affairs, education in the cities comes out of property taxes. There is no opportunity to control how those funds are used. This is a problem because secondary and post-secondary education is mostly off-reserve.

It was noted that the discussion had assumed continuing provincial control of education, rather than exploring the form that curriculum would take if Aboriginal people were in charge. A Métis participant said she was in favour of Indian control, but noted that her community would not be interested in another level of federal schools. She said Indian and Métis students should not be integrated into a single school system.

> There should be an Indian School Board in Regina, but the Métis would not be part of that; Métis and Indian are a separate people.

The discussion reached an impasse.

Participants agreed that Aboriginal parents need to control their children's education in urban areas. They agreed there needs to be a much greater degree of control of education by and accountability to Aboriginal urban parents. They agreed there needs to be more Aboriginal content in curriculum. They agreed these courses should be offered to all students, not just Aboriginal students.

Participants could not agree, however, on these proposals:

• Aboriginal membership on existing school boards;
• Aboriginal advisory councils for existing school boards;
• separate Aboriginal school boards;
• separate Indian, Métis and Inuit school boards in urban areas;
• federal, provincial or Aboriginal jurisdiction.

The participants recommended that

> The National Association of Friendship Centres, Assembly of First Nations, Métis National Council, and the Native Council of Canada should set up a consortium which would examine the potential of developing our own board for the study of Aboriginal education and accrediting programs without treading on the toes of the Department of Indian Affairs and Northern Development, any government funding, treaty rights, or the jurisdictions of various levels of government. This must be done also without sacrificing academic excellence, but it gives us control over our own education.

With respect to post-secondary education, the participants said that university entrance requirements should be challenged. As one participant pointed out, "It is possible to write a thesis in Micmac at one Maritime university."

In addition, participants felt that more money should be made available to Aboriginal students through business bursaries and grants, and that national Aboriginal organizations should lobby for more money for post-secondary education.

Housing

The participants were blunt about the urgent need for adequate and appropriate housing for Aboriginal people in urban centres.

> There is a desperate need for culturally appropriate housing in many cities.

Culturally appropriate housing for Aboriginal urban people is described as housing that is low-rent and may be Aboriginal-owned and -operated. It may include visits from elders or counselling programs for behavioral problems or substance abuse. The leases might have restrictions banning people who drink alcohol or take chemical substances. In short, such housing would form a mini-community for Aboriginal urban people seeking a safe, culturally appropriate environment in which to raise their children.

> This means housing of high quality. For instance, when we supply a home to get kids off the street, it must not be a place where alcoholism and other forms of abuse are permitted.

This kind of housing is becoming more sought after, although there are too few units by far to fill the need. The participants said the overwhelming priority is still to find enough adequate, liveable, clean housing for Aboriginal urban people – culturally appropriate or not.

> We need homes for our homeless men. Urban people need facilities, specifically a safe home.

Some of the other priorities identified by participants were as follows:

> Culturally appropriate, low-cost housing is a critical issue for Aboriginal students, who are scattered throughout the cities in which they live. Child care is another important concern.

> An Indian mother is grateful that her education is being paid for, but she needs affordable housing and day care. It is not just the homeless who need homes. Many people need housing run, staffed, owned and controlled by Aboriginal people.

Participants also suggested that

- The Canada Mortgage and Housing Corporation should provide support for student housing that could be owned and operated by Aboriginal people.
- Rent-to-own housing was identified as an important option.
- In some communities, the purchase of hotels for affordable housing has shown that people can do collectively what they might not be able to do individually.
- Mention was made of housing co-ops as solutions to urban housing problems and possibly as solutions for university students.

People with Disabilities

People with disabilities face special problems. Aboriginal people with disabilities, participants said, face these problems that are further compounded by cultural differences and the other problems faced by Aboriginal urban people.

In Alberta, a task force found there are several issues disabled people encounter: employment, education, financial support, personal issues, cultural isolation, transportation, housing, accessibility of services, and lack of information.

However, participants said, little priority is given to issues affecting Aboriginal people with disabilities. They said Aboriginal people with disabilities often move to the cities for treatment or to be closer to services. However, they confront different problems unique to urban centres.

Aboriginal urban people with disabilities find that

- accessible housing is scarce;
- adequate home care is difficult to find;
- transportation is difficult;
- social interaction is sharply curtailed;
- educational and training programs are not designed to accommodate people with disabilities or to meet their needs; and
- employment opportunities are scarce.

One participant said, "There must be more awareness among Aboriginal people about the needs of the disabled person. Aboriginal people with disabilities are marginalized. They lack an effective voice to press for services to meet their needs... In most cases, there is just no service available to the Aboriginal urban person with disabilities."

Aboriginal urban people with disabilities also face racism and experience abuse and violence. This participant said Aboriginal urban people have to care because no one else seems to.

> The disabled need respect, not pity. There was an urban disabled Native man who had his throat slashed – no one cares!

The participant said Aboriginal people with disabilities need to feel as useful and productive as everyone else. They need to upgrade their education to get training or retraining and jobs.

> Jobs are hard to come by in Saskatchewan. Many people with disabilities have only Grade 6 education. Social services does not allow them to go to school, and transportation is difficult. The solution here is to seek support services for education.

> People with physical disabilities need retraining. People who work for job strategy programs, the Workers Compensation Board, and every provincial agency should seek out people with disabilities.

Other participants said disabled Aboriginal people need services that are culturally appropriate. They, too, have experienced residential schools, racism and
poverty and like other Aboriginal people, have to deal with deep emotional and
spiritual hurt.

> Disabled people are forced to move to the city to receive treatment,
> but then find they must rely on services that follow non-Aboriginal
> models.

> The holistic approach to health and wellness is especially important
> for Aboriginal people with disabilities, many of whom were perma-
> nently injured in accidents arising from substance abuse or violence.

However, participants said few people are aware of the problems of the
Aboriginal person with disabilities because of the lack of information available.
One participant said that if statistics were kept on Aboriginal people with dis-
abilities, they would "support the need for services." They also said that
"Aboriginal people must become more aware of the needs of the disabled
Aboriginal urban person or those needs will continue to be ignored."

Justice

Participants made a direct connection between the cultural disruption in their
communities and the high percentage of Aboriginal people who are swept up by
the justice system. They spoke about building pride and self-esteem in young
Aboriginal people as a means of preventing the institutionalization of yet another generation. At present, participants said,

> These kids are programmed to graduate to jail... We need our own
> healing circles.

Participants said there is a need for Aboriginal counsellors to work in high
schools with large Aboriginal populations. They also said police, lawyers, judges
and parole officers need to consider alternatives and use discretion even before
young Aboriginal people become caught up in the justice system. They said
every attempt should be made to keep young Aboriginal people out of the justice system, if at all possible.

However, once young Aboriginal people do become involved with the justice
system, alternative measures should be considered to avoid incarceration or custody. Participants said police, lawyers and judges should be aware that at present, only six per cent enter the alternative sentencing program because the justice system does not consider alternatives to incarceration and custody.

In general, participants said, not enough attention is paid to the situation of
Aboriginal young offenders or their special problems. They mentioned the lack

of recreational facilities, employment and appropriate counselling programs in Aboriginal communities as conditions that promote a high incidence of involvement with the justice system among young Aboriginal people.

The participants also pointed to Aboriginal people's different perceptions of what constitute 'law' and 'justice'. Aboriginal societies believe in healing or restoring harmony, while

> The legal system tends to punish and institutionalize people, rather than providing treatment. There is no awareness that the symptoms addressed by incarceration have deeper roots.

That awareness does not seem to exist in the present justice system, participants said. Judges, lawyers and the police should be sensitized to Aboriginal culture and values. In dealing with Aboriginal young offenders, however, participants suggested that

> Elders must be involved in counselling young offenders, with their parents or grandparents present. Young people are the hope for the future, and are the largest single group in the Aboriginal population, so it makes sense to design special programs to meet their needs.

Alternative measures and counselling should be provided for adult offenders as well. Counselling, the participants said, must include the whole family, including the offender, especially in cases of family violence or sexual abuse. There must also be more half-way houses and programs to help the Aboriginal offender re-enter the community.

> The perpetrator must be at the centre of the treatment in order to deal with the problem holistically.

Participants said there are still problems with the way the justice system treats Aboriginal women. Jails for Aboriginal women often isolate them far from appropriate counselling and the support of family, children and friends. A new healing lodge announced by the federal government, for instance, "will be less accessible than was originally expected."

Some participants said, however, that although changes to the existing justice system could make it more sensitive and responsive to the needs of Aboriginal people, they want "their own court system based on traditional values, ethics and [justice] systems."

Other participants suggested that there be inquiries into the way provincial justice systems deal with Aboriginal people in all provinces, similar to those already held in Nova Scotia, Manitoba and Alberta.

Training

The participants said literacy, upgrading and job training programs for Aboriginal people in urban centres are underfunded, understaffed and inadequate. They cited long waiting lists and a scarcity of spaces as evidence of the urgent need for more programs, more funding and more Aboriginal staff.

Low levels of education among Aboriginal people are barriers to employment. They condemn Aboriginal urban people to poverty and dependence on social programs. Literacy, combined with life skills programs, were seen as a way to encourage Aboriginal people to upgrade their education, seek higher education and find employment.

Despite the proven need, the participants said there is a lack of support and funding from the federal government for literacy and skills training programs. Other participants identified the need for job retraining programs for Aboriginal people new to the urban job market. "Aboriginal people often find their skills are not transferable when they come to the city," said one delegate, citing heavy equipment operators and forestry workers as examples.

> Specific needs include life skills and literacy training. Program delivery should be based on partnerships with existing educational institutions and chambers of commerce.

> Literacy rates are another barrier to education.

One round table participant said that Aboriginal people do not have the same opportunities for jobs as counsellors with Aboriginal social services. The Aboriginal person may have taken all of the courses needed to do the job but may not have a degree. The person might have been doing the job for years. Participants said that experience should count for something, and they should be able to get the jobs. Yet, the Aboriginal person is often overlooked when a permanent staff position opens up or there is a conference to organize. Said one participant:

> Aboriginal people should have equal opportunities to act as facilitators at workshops and conferences. Their experience and insights should be recognized on a par with technical skills in a group process.

Another participant said, "Training programs delivered by Aboriginal people working for an Aboriginal service agency...have never been more important, but accreditation is an ongoing problem." The participant said it was a matter of control.

> You hire Aboriginal people because you want a program that is sensitive and knowledgeable to the needs of Aboriginal people. Because of

their low education, not too many have degrees, but you can train them. It becomes a truly Aboriginal program and a good one too. But, as a program manager, you wonder how you can obtain funding without staff who have received diplomas or certificates from institutions that are not geared to Aboriginal people. You can't.

The participant argued that when non-Aboriginal people with degrees were hired, the Aboriginal program necessarily becomes less 'Aboriginal', more like existing non-Aboriginal programs, and therefore less effective for its Aboriginal clients. The participant made this suggestion:

A number of excellent programs have been developed by experienced Aboriginal trainers, but they are not recognized by funders. The Nechi Institute in Alberta has trained 2,500 people over an 18-year period, but has had incredible difficulties obtaining provincial accreditation because the program was unwilling to give up Aboriginal control. One alternative would be to form a consortium of Aboriginal training institutions.

The participant said that Aboriginal training institutions should be able to train Aboriginal people and provide accreditation that equals or exceeds provincial standards. Many already provide that level of training. Participants said the example given shows what happens when ethnocentrism pervades social services programs and leads to the assumption that non-Aboriginal programs are automatically better or more legitimate than Aboriginal programs.

It also illustrates the problems caused by jurisdictional friction. "There aren't jurisdictional problems in getting funding, getting recognition or accreditation (caused by an overlap between federal and provincial jurisdiction); it is a jurisdictional void. Both sides want to say no to Aboriginal control without accepting responsibility for funding these programs." All of the participants said funding was a major problem in all service areas.

Elders

The participants described elders as an under-used resource in their communities. They said the influence of elders, as keepers of traditional Aboriginal knowledge and culture in their communities, had diminished over the years. The participants said the traditional role of elders had become less central to community life. As if to illustrate the point, some participants said there were more incidents of elder abuse being reported, perhaps as the issue became better known or better reported.

Some participants recalled a presentation made to the Royal Commission on the Aboriginal urban experience in Winnipeg. They said it identified twelve main barriers to the social, political and economic development in the Aboriginal urban population of that city. They said that list includes

> status of women, lack of involvement of youth and elders, and unwillingness of governing chiefs and tribal councils to see urban people as players in the discussion of self-government, among other concerns.

Participants said, however, that the relatively recent resurgence of traditional culture and values, and the reassertion of Aboriginal self-determination, have made the role of elders more vital and necessary. As a consequence, elders are now seen as a 'new' resource.

> In some smaller communities, elders are emerging as a relatively new resource. In at least one city, elders sit on the sentencing panel for young offenders.

The participants described the role of elders in terms that went beyond mere volunteers performing a public service. Elders, they implied, provide spiritual guidance as well. Their status within Aboriginal communities is often unacknowledged or ignored, however, by non-Aboriginal authorities or agencies. One participant gave this example:

> Elders are supposed to have the same rights as chaplains, but they have been forced to work in isolation from other advisers. Elders should be a part of the entire prison process, including parole.

However, the most vital role of elders, according to participants, is in the area of education and instructing young Aboriginal people about traditional values and culture. Here too, however, participants said elders are not always respected.

> Elders aren't invited into schools very often. Schools have rigid notions of who should be allowed in to speak.

Participants said the role of elders in Aboriginal urban society must be acknowledged by both Aboriginal and non-Aboriginal people as providing important if not invaluable services to the community. They are treated as volunteers for little pay and less recognition. Their contributions should be recognized. At the very least, one participant said, "Elders must receive fair pay for their services."

Recommendations

Many recommendations came out of the services workshops, some controversial, some effectively neutral. Still others were stated with matter-of-fact conviction that prompted consensus rather than discussion. In highlighted form, this is what the Commission heard:

- The overall level of services in urban areas is inadequate and should be substantially improved.

- Aboriginal urban people must take control of both the development and the implementation of services.
- Aboriginal people must not establish systems that recreate barriers and carry on their own internal oppression.
- The question of who delivers services must be resolved.
- The federal government must recognize and address mental health issues in urban areas.
- People's learning and life experiences must be recognized and valued in hiring decisions.
- Aboriginal people must have the opportunity to establish their own standards of service – and it must be recognized that those standards will almost always exceed those established by non-Aboriginal organizations.
- Accreditation must be provided for educational programs that reflect the needs of Aboriginal urban populations, not the bureaucratic needs of institutions that support assimilation, and more Aboriginal content must be incorporated into history and Canadian studies for all students.
- Successful models in rural communities should be explored in urban areas, to avoid reinventing the wheel.
- Urban people need better communication with their communities of origin as a means of sensitizing leaders to urban issues and preventing people from falling between the cracks.
- Program development must be based on consumers' needs.
- Educational institutions for Aboriginal youth and adults must address issues of self-esteem.
- The portability of treaty rights, with specific emphasis on DIAND's curtailment of social services for out-of-province First Nations, needs to be addressed.
- Service needs in urban areas are bound to increase with the influx of people from reserves. Young people in the city are dropping out of school every day, underscoring the need for a national indigenous youth council with strong roots in both the urban areas and the reserves.

Health and Wellness

General Statements

Participants in the several workshops on this topic summarized some of the problems in their particular urban centres as follows:

- financial,
- low self-esteem,
- lack of services,
- violence (general/familial),
- substance abuse,
- lack of family services,
- abuse in boarding schools and other institutionalized situations,
- sexual, mental and spiritual abuse,
- divided jurisdiction, and
- lack of culturally sensitive health services and lack of access to health services generally.

Participants agreed there is a lack of support for Aboriginal people in general, lack of cultural and traditional awareness for urban families, lack of leadership among urban communities, and a lack of cohesiveness between Inuit, Métis and Status people. Participants' comments show there is some agreement not only on the issues facing Aboriginal urban people but also in perceptions of what is required for health and well-being.

Simply put, Aboriginal people do not equate the adequacy of service delivery or the amount of services provided with their people's security, health and wellness. The delegates repeatedly expressed the need for services to provide for the spiritual, emotional and psychological needs of Aboriginal urban people. These needs, they said, were equal in importance with meeting physical needs in promoting health and wellness in their communities. In fact, they considered this approach essential to the future well-being of their communities.

> The large number of Aboriginal people that are institutionalized is of great concern. When institutionalization is within families it causes a lack of parenting. We do not learn parenting skills in an institutional setting; this produces dysfunctional families. This happens in urban and rural settings. This becomes your culture, you are used to it.

One participant explained that there have been, and continue to be, repeated disruptions of Aboriginal communities by various outside authorities. These disruptions have affected the passing on of parenting skills among successive generations of Aboriginal people. Many Aboriginal parents feel they are no longer able to teach their children the values and appropriate behaviours of their societies and, therefore, they feel ill-equipped to ensure the mental, spiritual and emotional well-being of their children. Children, as the delegate explained, have grown up in dysfunctional families and are now producing dysfunctional families of their own.

This is not a problem confined only to Aboriginal families and communities, one delegate explained. It is a Canadian problem. The products of dysfunctional Aboriginal families and communities grow up institutionalized, by the child welfare system, by the justice system, by the social service system. They migrate to urban centres. They are a Canadian problem.

> There is a lack of identity. Aboriginal children are apprehended, adopted out, and they don't realize their connections. As children grow older and their Aboriginal features appear, the adopted society shuns them.

> Aboriginal children are often left with no value system at all, because they have not had Aboriginal values passed on and have nobody helping them learn those mainstream values. There is also a lack of cultural awareness among government personnel and child care workers.

Participants gave examples of men "who go to jail by choice. One went to get his teeth fixed; one went back to play ball, since it was all he knew and it gave him recognition." One woman spoke of children who stay in the child welfare system because they need braces.

The delegates defined problems that are buried deep within their families, cultures and communities. They described violence of all forms. They spoke of child and sexual abuse. They talked of the loss of individual and cultural identity, low self-esteem, joblessness, institutional dependency and a lack of self-confidence, homelessness, addictions, suicide and AIDS.

Prostitution

Delegates said they considered prostitution both an issue of exploitation of poor, young Aboriginal men and women and an issue of cultural degradation. They felt stronger laws are needed to punish the people exploiting young Aboriginal people – the pimps and the johns. They also felt that more must be done to provide economic alternatives and counselling to Aboriginal youth involved in prostitution to raise their self-esteem and help them gain a positive self-image.

They also said that alternatives were needed. Long-term solutions should be based on jobs and job skills development. Short-term solutions include rehabilitation for addictions, prevention from disease through needle exchange, and safe places to meet the needs of young prostitutes. Service providers should go to the people; mobile vans were identified as one program option. It is equally important to develop a network of resources in the community, or the youth will inevitably return to the street.

Another participant said many prostitutes were sexually abused as children and are often from foster care situations. Aboriginal children need to be kept safe while on the street, but they must also be protected before looking to the streets for what should be provided at home.

> For prostitutes, pimps act as part of an extended family on the street. Girls begin idolizing the pimps, who provide security and safety for them. There is a sense of order, because the pimps have their territory and they regulate each other.

There is a need to reach kids before they turn to prostitution by developing culturally sensitive services that offer alternatives to prostitution. The delegates said many Aboriginal youth who turn to prostitution do so for financial reasons. Training and more jobs would mean fewer Aboriginal adolescents turning to prostitution.

> Women who want to be independent would sooner be prostitutes than receive welfare. Welfare represents dependence. There are different levels of prostitution, the protected form of escort services and the unprotected prostitution on the street.

Violence

A friendship centre worker said violence occurs mostly in situations where alcohol is being abused. She pointed to the lack of support systems in communities, where courts and RCMP are not supportive. In fact, she said, women victims are seen to be at fault or are thought to have 'asked for it'. Women who come together to oppose violence are seen as feminists and radicals.

The issue of violence is not understood very well in Aboriginal communities. The delegates recognized that violence in many forms – family violence, sexual abuse, child abuse and wife battering – is prevalent throughout Aboriginal communities. The reasons are disputed. The suggested solutions were not forthcoming. Instead of addressing the issue of violence, the delegates could only agree on how to rescue the victims and try to treat the victimizers.

Participants spoke about establishing more shelters for battered women, more counselling for children victimized by violence, and counselling for men as victimizers. But delegates spoke about violence as a way of life, as a means of venting frustration and a signal of despair. They also spoke about years of being ordered to keep silent about the violence, both as victims and as victimizers.

> After I gave a talk about family violence and abuse, a nun stood up and objected for making her feel sad and said those things never happened. The Church is afraid to say anything.

> Child, sexual, and elder abuse is common, but not talked about. Communities won't admit there is a problem, even when the information is gathered and shows it's a big problem. One issue never talked about is child sexual abuse, it's a taboo to talk about such a thing. In most communities, everyone says 'shhh!, don't talk about it.'

Today, violence in its many forms is becoming better known as people become more aware of the problem. People are being encouraged to talk about the violence. However, the delegates admitted that many people get mixed messages: on the one hand, they're told it is best to report acts of violence; on the other hand, they fear the traumatic disruption of their lives and family relationships.

> Children know the abuse is wrong, but fear they will break up the family if they talk about it. They blame themselves, they feel guilty. Children are not talking about it, they don't know how to talk about the abuse. It's related to how children are taught how to talk in school.

Participants expressed concern about violence, not only as a problem with adults, but with children who are learning violent ways of coping with problems. Violence is a learned behaviour, one commented. Aboriginal adults and children need to learn positive ways to deal with anger.

> I had a violent family – a violent mum, a violent dad, and violent brothers. I was a student of violence. As I grew up, I became exactly like them.

Poverty, lack of work, and hopelessness contribute to violence, but the bottom line is fear, the delegates said. Fear is behind the violence. Fear allows it to continue. Fear prevents people from doing something to stop the cycle of violence. Participants said, for example, women withdraw charges against their abusers at the last minute because they are afraid of not being believed or of the consequences if they are.

Specifically, delegates said, there must be greater efforts to inform people about violence and its consequences. They said that people need to know that there is support for the victims of abuse and violence through counselling, safe homes and – if need be – legal sanctions. But they also said that victims must understand that they have to stop being 'victims' and assume control over their own lives.

Speakers denounced the lack of facilities for abuse victims in Aboriginal communities. "As a Métis person, I wouldn't know where to go," said one person. Another noted the lack of facilities for Métis people, emphasizing that Métis culture is different from First Nations cultures.

Speakers noted Aboriginal people need more information about how to get out of abusive situations. This should include talking to survivors of abuse. "As an abused woman you feel you don't have a voice," one woman said. "Men need to accept responsibility and admit they have a problem, and it must be remembered that men in rehabilitation are there as part of their sentencing, rather than voluntarily."

The delegates also recommended the establishment of a 24-hour hot-line in friendship centres. They also need trained counsellors to work as crisis intervention workers and counsellors to help people resume their lives and recover from the trauma of violence.

Mental Health

Participants connected emotional stability and the absence of behavioural problems in individuals and the community with strong cultural and traditional values.

> Mental health has nothing to do with being crazy. If people have a strong feeling of their culture, they don't have mental health problems.

In keeping with this observation, many participants associated the general level of well-being of Aboriginal people and their communities with the cultural disruption and erosion that has occurred. Conversely, emotional instability in an individual was seen as a sign of low self-esteem, poor self-image, and a weak or non-existent sense of Aboriginal identity.

Participants saw several reasons for this situation: a long history of attempts by churches and non-Aboriginal governments to assimilate Aboriginal people and efforts to wipe out Aboriginal languages, destroy Aboriginal religions, dismiss Aboriginal social and political institutions, and remove from the individual any vestige of Aboriginal culture and traditional values.

Participants referred to repeated intrusions into their societies by outside authorities to remove their children and place them in institutions with the aim of assimilation. Chief among these were church-run residential schools.

Participants spoke about decades of assimilation and the effect of these forced removals of Aboriginal children on their families, communities and societies. They described the products of the residential school system as 'damaged' people – people who were left culturally, spiritually and emotionally damaged if not crippled. Aboriginal people today, they said, are left to bear the burden and to deal with the damage.

> It will be a long time before students of residential schools are past child-bearing age. In B.C., the last residential schools only closed ten years ago. Now children are being raised by parents who have residential school as a long-term experience. It will be another two generations before the residential school experience begins to fade.

The residential schools were not the only intrusions into Aboriginal communities. Non-Aboriginal social workers removed thousands of children from their families and cultures to place them in the child welfare system. The justice system today performs much the same function and on a similar scale. The institutionalization of several generations of Aboriginal people, damaging the ability of culture and the community to function or survive, was identified by participants as the predominant factor underlying many of the social problems in Aboriginal communities today.

It is only recently, said one participant, that Aboriginal people have been able to begin to deal with the problems of institutionalization and of the residential school syndrome. However, he said, efforts by the Aboriginal community to heal itself are hindered by the apparent refusal by non-Aboriginal professionals and governments to acknowledge the nature or the degree of the problem. He spoke about the emerging 'residential school syndrome' and the lack of services to deal with it.

> What do we do when we say we need a psychiatrist or psychologist or when we need a medicine man to work with someone? There are no professionals from our own communities in these fields.

Participants said that counselling programs in urban centres are not culturally appropriate. These programs and similar models may be equipped to deal with problems in non-Aboriginal society but they have little relevance to the specific problems of Aboriginal people. One participant noted that

> ...psychologists cannot deal with our problems, they cannot see our culture clearly. They see us from a European, white, point of view.

Along with the underlying problems stemming from cultural disruption, Aboriginal people have to deal with cultural dislocation. They move to the cities for many reasons but they find themselves beset by new and unfamiliar problems and pressures. One person described the anxiety in this way:

> The bigger Winnipeg gets, the greater the sense of isolation for Natives, the less they practise togetherness. It is very difficult to 'feel' Native culture in the urban areas. In the rural areas Natives are in closer touch with one another.

Others leave their rural communities, whether by choice or necessity, and find there is no culturally appropriate service or treatment available for them once they arrive in urban centres.

> Some people have to leave the reserves with mental health problems because they are pushed off. To get rid of the problem, they are sent away. Since these people need constant attention, and the communities cannot deal with them, they end up in hospitals with very few Native doctors and nurses.

Aboriginal people are refused access to funding to set up and run their own mental health programs because of jurisdictional problems.

> Mental health is a provincial matter, so communities have had no access to federal funds. There are no Native agencies that handle mental health.

Another participant said some Aboriginal emergency counselling programs in urban centres are operated by volunteers and are not always open.

> There are some that are open from 9 a.m. to 5 p.m. but not on weekends, so you must plan your breakdown!

Considering the scope of the problem and the dire need for appropriate services, participants said there must be a national effort to provide mental health services to Aboriginal people. Participants insisted the effort must be holistic because of the nature and degree of the problems in their communities.

> It must not be a piecemeal effort. Mental health is important, but issues like welfare, education, and child well-being are equally important. You will get piecemeal cures unless issues are considered together with the family unit as the focus.

There are appropriate models that governments could use, one participant said. The participant had visited Australia and saw a program that worked well.

> There was a counselling program that treated the whole family, not just the individual. The family lived with 12 other families on 60 acres of land. The results were good because the whole family was treated. More of this whole family counselling is needed.

Participants noted, however, that healing circles already exist in some Aboriginal communities. This concept needs to be expanded and extended. Other models might come forth if the government made efforts to support them. The problem most participants agreed is that

> A Native mental health policy needs to be set up; there are 20 principles as identified through a national group. These are recommenda-

tions to build a framework on for programs. Métis and Indian mental health programs can be negotiated with both federal and provincial governments. Aboriginal people presently working in Indian and Métis mental health must be included in any government policy-making group.

HIV and AIDS

Participants focused on AIDS and HIV realizing these are important, sensitive health issues that cut deep into the attitudes of Aboriginal urban people. They are topics that, as one participant said, people do not want to deal with:

> Often AIDS doesn't become an issue until someone experiences the death of someone close.

Participants blamed fear and ignorance of the disease, as well as a tendency by everyone to avoid an uncomfortable subject. While shouldering some of the blame for not doing enough themselves,

> There is a lot of denial around AIDS. Québec has no Aboriginal AIDS program, although the Montreal friendship centre has begun distributing condoms and training staff. Vancouver is expanding its program.

> It is difficult in Alberta to get the message across about AIDS; for example, an in-service session on AIDS for staff and board members only attracted three participants. AIDS should be on the agenda at the monthly, provincial advisory meetings.

They also blamed governments for failing to get information about HIV and AIDS into Aboriginal communities.

> The AIDS epidemic has raised such a high level of fear that many people have been unable to discuss the need for prevention and treatment. The combination of ignorance, isolation, and lack of serious investment from governments could turn the epidemic into a disaster for Aboriginal populations. A participant said 73 per cent of the people who use the needle exchange program in Winnipeg, and 63 per cent in Calgary, are of Aboriginal origin. Street workers are frustrated that this issue has not received higher priority. Many people are involved in self-destructive behaviour, and there is a misconception that First Nations are immune to AIDS.

Participants said they weren't sure how to get beyond the denial that exists in Aboriginal communities. Very often, they would approach elders in their communities for advice or direction. A participant noted, however, that some elders often find discussion of sexual matters uncomfortable. The participants explained that in order to broach sexual matters with some elders, they had to invent euphemisms.

Participants deplored the lack of culturally appropriate programs related to AIDS and the non-existence of AIDS treatment programs and hospices designed specifically for Aboriginal people living with AIDS. One participant suggested that

> Existing AIDS programs should be used, but they should include an Aboriginal component.

This person was in the minority, however. Most participants agreed that Aboriginal people should run AIDS programs for Aboriginal people. This included awareness programs, treatment programs and the establishment and administration of Aboriginal AIDS hospices.

> Aboriginal people living with AIDS in urban settings need their own treatment facility. They should not have to go to mainstream facilities for the specialized services they require.

> Health promotion must also include AIDS awareness. AIDS hospices must be run by Aboriginal people.

> On the topic of AIDS awareness, friendship centres need to be actively involved. Friendship centres are the first places people go when they come off the reserve. They require funding and resources; pilot programs should not be a hardship on the centres. The elected leaders should be interested in the AIDS issue and be able to provide strong directives that the centres should abide by. The National Association of Friendship Centres should provide direction.

Participants noted that the Medical Services Branch of the federal Department of Health and Welfare has an Aboriginal AIDS awareness program but that it is aimed at First Nations people living on-reserve. They said this program should be broadened to include the Aboriginal urban population as well and that federal and provincial governments should meet with Aboriginal leaders to develop a national Aboriginal AIDS policy.

Youth

The participants said services for youth are "too few" and "too rigid" and "tend to intimidate" the very people they are supposed to serve – Aboriginal youth. They said groups delivering services often overlook the needs of young Aboriginal people. When they do have youth programs, these are often of limited success. Participants described the situation as ultimately "frustrating".

They said the problems of Aboriginal youth in urban centres are enormous. Participants said a high percentage of the people using needle exchange programs in cities like Edmonton and Vancouver are Aboriginal youth. They said many young Aboriginal urban people are homeless, living on the streets from day to day, and these youth are often involved in prostitution, drugs and violence. Participants spoke in terms of "surviving" on the streets rather than living on the streets.

> I live on the streets. I don't know how the government agency works. We steal to survive. I'm working now, part time, but I want to improve my life. But it's hard out there. We do what we have to do to survive on the street. And we learn more bad things in the jails.

Many Aboriginal young people, participants said, are facing the same situations as their older counterparts: cultural confusion, a sense of lost identity, high unemployment, violence, racism and substance abuse. They also described Aboriginal youth as experiencing much higher rates of teen pregnancies, sexually transmitted diseases, HIV and AIDS, than other Canadians. They said many young people wind up living on the streets in urban centres "because of abusive situations at home." One participant described people, "as young as fourteen years old" dying with needles in their arms.

Like their older counterparts, young Aboriginal urban youth in urban centres have few programs to support them or meet their needs. One workshop facilitator suggested that street people "need a needle exchange program, condom use instruction and sex education in general", with an emphasis on reaching Aboriginal street youth. Some delegates disagreed, however, saying:

> We need to educate on growth and development, she said, rather than sex education. Teach them how to reach womanhood, manhood, wherever they are, because often when people relocate to the city they don't know who they are.

Participants recognized that attention is needed to provide emergency services for youth, aimed at improving their living conditions as well as preventive measures, aimed more at healing the individual. The participants described preventive measures such as these:

> ...education, sport, health, AIDS awareness, sex education, and recreation. Unemployment is a huge problem; the solution is to help students stay in school, complete high school, and get whatever training they need to begin a successful career. Young people must be raised to feel comfortable with their Aboriginal identity, and must grow up with pride, self-esteem and a desire to excel. Non-Aboriginal organizations must commit themselves to hiring larger numbers of Aboriginal people...

Other participants said Aboriginal youth need immediate help in the form of services that, most often, do not exist in many urban centres.

> A large number of street youth are involved in prostitution, and there are no services waiting for them when they are ready to leave the street.

They identified a similar lack of programs for Aboriginal youth trying to kick drugs or alcohol or just trying to upgrade their education or skills to get a job. They feared funding cutbacks in the few existing services for Aboriginal urban youth and they blamed the lack of funding and the lack of services on a void in federal, provincial and civic jurisdictions.

> Many street youth have no awareness of their culture or traditions. Many young people in Regina are falling through the cracks because of gaps between federal and provincial mandates, combined with a huge population influx from the reserves.

Consistently, participants associated the lack of recreational facilities and programs as the primary reason for addictive and criminal activity in young people. If recreational activities existed, they existed for older people who had the financial resources to be self-entertaining. Friendship centres were seen as the primary source of collective recreation but were seriously hampered in their efforts to provide recreation because "Unfortunately, recreational sports programming doesn't generate a lot of revenue for us."

But when young people find neither employment nor recreation, they have a greater tendency to use mind altering substances to alleviate their boredom and depression. Participants questioned how unlimited resources could be found to incarcerate Aboriginal young people but not to provide recreation and sport to steer them away from incarceration. In addition, beyond the resourcing issue, many participants felt that adults must be more involved and willing to donate freely of their time, knowledge, experience and resources to develop young people's interest and skill in sport. Sport and recreation were viewed as essential to developing self-esteem and healthy lifestyles.

They suggested that there should be more long-term recovery programs for young Aboriginal urban people ("not drop-in centres or detox centres") designed and run by Aboriginal people, including Aboriginal youth. There need to be more group homes under Aboriginal control and more cultural education in schools.

Participants also said there must be more employment training and a greater emphasis on meeting employment equity targets for Aboriginal people.

Children

Participants identified several issues concerning Aboriginal children. They said there was a lack of adequate – let alone culturally appropriate – daycare. They said Aboriginal urban children suffer from low self-esteem even at an early age as a result of the negative images impressed upon them by the educational system and the media. Children are confused about their cultural identity. The child welfare system is foreign and insensitive. Participants called the issues concerning Aboriginal urban children "monumental".

Participants said Aboriginal children are profoundly and adversely affected by the impoverished social conditions in their communities. Some participants cited the growing number of Aboriginal people relying on food banks and the incidence of children arriving at schools poorly clothed and hungry. They condemned the lack of lunch programs in urban schools. One participant said that his province "subsidizes liquor in northern communities, but not milk."

The participants said there was a connection between the social and cultural disruptions in families and communities and the incidence of low self-esteem on the part of Aboriginal children at an early age. However, they saved most of their criticism for the education system and the child welfare system.

Participants said these institutions intrude into the lives of Aboriginal parents, and the parents are often judged inadequate simply because they are Aboriginal. They said these institutions are not sensitive to their situations or responsive to their needs. Nor are they accountable to Aboriginal urban people. They said there are few Aboriginal people on school boards, and there are no mandated Aboriginal child welfare agencies in urban centres. Participants said this must change.

Aboriginal parents must have the same rights that other parents take for granted when it comes to the education of their children. They need to be able to support or question school policies, officials and teachers. They need to be able to examine the materials used by teachers in educating Aboriginal children.

There was little disagreement among participants when it came to the issue of child welfare. Participants said there must be mandated, Aboriginal-run, child welfare agencies in urban centres. They said Aboriginal parents must have some means of checking the broad, intrusive powers given to existing non-Aboriginal child welfare agencies. In other words, participants said, Aboriginal urban parents must have the fundamental right and the power to care for and protect their own children.

This power, they also said, must reside in the hands of Aboriginal urban parents. There are Aboriginal-run child welfare agencies on many reserves and in Métis communities, but some participants said they did not want these extended to cover Aboriginal urban families and children. These agencies had to be directly accountable to Aboriginal urban parents.

Aboriginal children who have been adopted out need counselling services, and so do their birth and adoptive parents. Participants also said there needs to be greater support for repatriation of adopted children sent out-of-province or out-of-country. The children must be given a chance to return and be reintegrated into their own cultures, if they wish.

Elders

A delegate said that the role of elders and of their special place in Aboriginal societies is neither recognized nor respected by non-Aboriginal society. He said elders not only counsel people on cultural, spiritual or emotional matters; in some cases they are healers of physical ailments as well. As such, he said they are similar to medical doctors or psychiatrists and they should be recognized by the medical community.

> The underlying problem is the interaction of an oral culture and a written culture. We have no papers or letters or exams, but the health care system works within these parameters, causing a problem for most medical people. The community endorses our elders but there is no certification process that non-Aboriginal society or culture can relate to.

One participant explained the traditional Aboriginal concept of health having four components: physical, mental, emotional and spiritual. Aboriginal people consider each component as important as the others and therefore have a holistic approach to health that is not reflected in the current medical services delivery system. Another speaker said centres capable of delivering the four components should be established in major cities across Canada. One woman responded to this suggestion with enthusiasm, saying she could come in for pregnancy care and then for help with parenting skills later. They said elders would need to play a central role in all of these services.

They also said elders must be allowed to act as ambassadors of Aboriginal cultures and societies. They must be allowed and encouraged to visit schools to teach Aboriginal children about cultural values and traditions. They said non-Aboriginal children should be allowed to participate as well. This is another way of combatting racism and negative stereotypes, delegates said.

Elders must be funded just as other programs are funded, some participants said. There must be more healing circles established in all urban centres. Elders should be paid a salary, delegates said. "It's not fair," one delegate stated, "that elders work for nothing. They volunteer and spend a lot of their own money. They should at least be compensated for their efforts."

Racism/Discrimination

Participants said racism and discrimination against Aboriginal people in urban centres is "pervasive". They said Aboriginal people face racial discrimination every day, in every urban centre, on the streets, at work, and sometimes at home. They said Aboriginal people experience violent attacks of a racist nature daily across the country. They said racism is so prevalent that many Aboriginal people simply accept violent racism and racial discrimination as a "normal" fact of life.

> Racism is a pervasive problem for Aboriginal people in urban settings. In Montreal, for example, 15 Inuit were located in a "psychotic ward" to isolate them from the racism around them.

Participants blamed attitudes for racist behaviour and policy. They said these attitudes are widespread and ingrained. Participants also blamed negative stereotypes conveyed through books, taught in schools, and reported on the evening news.

> There should be better textbooks in Aboriginal and non-Aboriginal schools. Some books should be banned, because they depict Natives as "greasy, boozing people" or "as nomads who live in tents." This image permeates the Aboriginal self-image, particularly Aboriginal urban people who lack contact with their own culture.

Participants said these widely accepted stereotypes and prejudice against Aboriginal people affect their self-esteem and buttress the barriers that prevent them from making improvements in their private lives and in their communities.

> There is no way for Aboriginal people to progress in the face of daily frustrations arising from prejudice. Substance abuse is caused by the low self-esteem that grows out of constant racism.

Participants said that much of the discrimination Aboriginal people face is institutional and systemic. They said that trained and qualified Aboriginal people "aren't being hired" and so they aren't represented on boards and in positions that deal with Aboriginal people on a regular basis.

> We end up with institutional racism where employees of a system do not have an emotional relationship with the Aboriginal people they deal with in jails, courts. Aboriginal people should be the ones to choose the people they want to represent them.

> The recession has fuelled discrimination and there has been a resurgence of a "redneck" attitude, especially in the cities.

Participants said more must be done to identify barriers to employment and economic development and to remove stereotypical images in school books, television and the other media. They said governments must raise the issue – if not attempt to change – society's attitudes toward Aboriginal people. They suggested a national campaign aimed at this goal.

The subject of institutional racism raised questions of whether existing institutions are appropriate for future use by Aboriginal people. For instance, they wondered whether institutions designed for colonialism, based on attitudes that presumed Aboriginal inferiority, were valid models for adaptation to more autonomous Aboriginal institutions. One participant put the question in terms of political development:

> Institutional racism is an important factor that leads to the question of whether existing institutions are suitable for Aboriginal people.

"Have we learned enough today to be able to develop institutions to serve Indian people?" a participant asked.

Participants also discussed internal Aboriginal racism and discrimination. They discussed discrimination by Aboriginal people against Aboriginal women, gay Aboriginal men and lesbians and people belonging to other Aboriginal groups.

> Fair-skinned Métis people face discrimination within the Aboriginal community, as do women married to non-Aboriginal men on reserves.

> ..it depends on the colour of your skin whether you really feel accepted in any kind of Native agency. For me, it does. It depends on what your name is. It depends on where you're from. Who you know. When I went to the Native Employment Services...with my sister, and my sister is, well, we dye our hair, and my sister is really blonde. So we went in there and we said we wanted an appointment and they said: Well, you have to be Native, you know. We said, we're Métis. What do we have to do? Carry our cards around or what? And it's like that all over Winnipeg...

Participants said Aboriginal people had "accepted the oppression" imposed upon them. Aboriginal people must overcome internal racism within Aboriginal societies, they said, which stems from the legal definitions and divisions imposed upon them by laws such as the *Indian Act*. These divisions, they said, "pit Indian against Métis" in the quest for government funds. The divisions allow Aboriginal people to accept and participate in discrimination when people seek services. Some participants said Aboriginal people need cross-cultural training about other Aboriginal groups just as much as other Canadians do.

Participants wondered whether a change of existing laws or creating new anti-racism laws to combat Aboriginal/non-Aboriginal racism would be effective.

> You can force someone to conform to a standard, but how can you change the way they think.

Others said tougher application of anti-racism laws, anti-discrimination laws, and more policies such as employment equity were the only ways to make real change. Doubt was expressed, however, that anything would change without legislation. Police and schools will not change willingly, participants said.

On the matter of internal Aboriginal racism and discrimination, some participants suggested removing divisions between Aboriginal urban people imposed by the *Indian Act* and giving all Aboriginal urban groups equal access to "one big pot of funding" and to services – on a status-blind basis. They said it was the only solution that could work in urban centres. However, participants failed to reach consensus on specific recommendations to combat the attitudes that allow internal Aboriginal racism and discrimination to persist.

Recommendations

A greater degree of unanimity was apparent in the health and wellness workshops. Participants were clear about what was needed and how it was to be done. Although there was some disagreement about the merit of the status-blind approach, many recommendations had the support of the substantial majority.

- There is a need for a tripartite process involving Aboriginal communities and federal and provincial governments to eliminate jurisdictional problems and get dollars flowing for Aboriginal services. Most problems and blockages in the area of health and wellness arise from jurisdictional issues.
- Aboriginal people must be empowered to put forward their own definition of health and wellness. Elders must be empowered to work in collaboration with western medicine.
- Aboriginal people health and wellness centres must be controlled and operated by Aboriginal people. The Aboriginal approach to health is reflected in a concern with prevention, rather than treatment of disease.
- There is a need for Aboriginal unity around health issues.

- Programs that emphasize education, sport, AIDS awareness, sex education, and recreation for young people should be initiated or strengthened.
- Greater support is needed to help students stay in school, complete high school, and get whatever training they need to begin a successful career.
- Young people must be raised to feel comfortable with their Aboriginal identity, and must grow up with pride, self-esteem and a desire to excel.
- Non-Aboriginal organizations must commit themselves to hiring larger numbers of Aboriginal people.
- The federal government must recognize that we have a Third World country right here that needs a portion of what currently goes to developing countries internationally.
- There should be a national campaign aimed at changing society's attitude toward Aboriginal people with accompanying tougher anti-racism legislation.
- Greater outreach efforts are required such as mobile service limits which go to people on the street to offer a needle exchange program, condom use instruction or sex education in general.
- Prevention in the form of family support must be the first step in reducing adolescent prostitution.
- Strengthening cultural pride and participation was commonly thought to be the priority solution for mental health problems and low self-esteem.
- Twenty-four hour, seven-days-a-week crisis services need to be established.
- Services must be holistic.
- The AIDS program currently funded by Medical Services Branch should be extended to service more urban areas.
- Elders should be encouraged to participate in Aboriginal and provincial educational system.
- Stereotypical images of Aboriginal people must be banned from text book material and media presentation.
- There is an immediate need to establish status-blind service centres in the nine major service centres across Canada (Vancouver, Toronto, Winnipeg, Montreal, Calgary, Edmonton, Halifax, Saskatoon, Regina). The meaning of "status-blind" and "level playing field" received a lot of discussion, with priority placed on the re-establishment of an Aboriginal 'family' in which all have a place.
- Racism within the Aboriginal community must be addressed by movement away from legal definitions of who is and who is not Aboriginal.
- There must be more employment training and a greater emphasis on meeting employment equity targets for Aboriginal people.

- There must be mandated, Aboriginal-run, child welfare agencies in urban centres. Aboriginal parents must have some means of checking the broad, intrusive powers given to existing non-Aboriginal child welfare agencies.

Economics

General Statements

As in the other workshops, delegates did not see economic issues existing in isolation from other issues in their communities. Instead, they perceived the potential for success or failure of economic and employment development in their communities as being connected with the spiritual and cultural well-being in those same communities. Economic development was perceived as a tool to help Aboriginal people rebuild their communities and societies. A healthier Aboriginal community might then be able to sustain itself with increased economic investment and employment opportunities in the future.

Although many of the delegates identified specific issues, problems and barriers to economic and employment opportunities in Aboriginal urban communities, many noted that there could be little accomplished in terms of improving the economic development of Aboriginal communities unless social and cultural issues were addressed simultaneously.

Some of the barriers to economic improvement they identified were the following:

- low education and literacy levels;
- a lack of job training programs;
- inadequate funding for upgrading and literacy programs;
- poor social conditions;
- chronic high unemployment rates;
- ineffective employment equity programs; and
- a lack of child care for single parents.

Many of the delegates identified racism as the number one barrier to the improvement of economic opportunities in Aboriginal urban communities.

> Racism in government, business, and in the community in general is...systemic.

> Current programs maintain the problems rather than solving them. It's a revolving door. The programs seem to suit the government, and there is an inequity in programs for Aboriginal people versus the non-Aboriginal population. For example, a new program like employment equity is countered with new rules for entry.

Programs aimed at improving the situation were seen by delegates as ineffective.

> Program development and delivery has taken place with no community involvement. The result is that services are irrelevant to the needs of Aboriginal urban communities and are not culturally appropriate.

> Some common problems are a lack of funding for programs, a lack of control over programs and a lack of flexibility.

> The programs don't reflect cultural needs and are no more than a band-aid solution.

Participants cited jurisdictional problems, saying that Aboriginal urban people are excluded from federal programs offered to on-reserve populations. They said they are effectively excluded from benefiting from mainstream economic development initiatives because federal programs exist for Aboriginal people and, therefore, they are a federal responsibility. The problems and complaints were so familiar to some of the people that they expressed frustration that the discussion was taking such a familiar turn. The problems are well known, but there has never been any follow-up.

In summarizing the discussion, participants did, however, identify certain measures to be taken in order to increase economic development activity in urban centres.

- increased accessibility to development programs;
- accountability;
- acquisition of real estate to house Aboriginal people, businesses and organizations;
- training and empowerment;
- development of technical, managerial and political expertise;
- efforts to counter bureaucratic barriers;
- establishment of partnerships among Aboriginal businesses, politicians and educators to pool resources;
- ethical, efficient management;
- joint ventures between reserves, settlements, and nearby Aboriginal urban communities;
- linkages between culture and economic development; and
- sustainable funding.

Economic Development

There are too few Aboriginal-owned and -operated businesses, and little is known about those that do exist. There are too few investment dollars for Aboriginal businesses and training or internship programs to allow young Aboriginal people to graduate into business.

These are but a few of the issues raise by participants with respect to the way development of new business and job creation is handled in Aboriginal urban communities.

Participants said that funding was inadequate and is breeding an industry of dependence rather than building self-reliance in Aboriginal urban communities. Communities have no input into program design, no control over allocations, and no say in the use of money once it is allocated. They said Aboriginal people have trouble getting loans, providing collateral and getting government support, especially for small Aboriginal businesses. As one participant explained:

> It cost me $30.00 to make a pair of moccasins but I had to sell them for $20 because I needed the money. If I had had financing, I could have waited and sold six pairs for $50 apiece.

Collateral is often a necessary part of obtaining a business loan, but many Aboriginal people have very little collateral. Participants suggested that perhaps Aboriginal people could start their own credit unions or establish their own financial institutions. Others suggested an investment and development program based on the Calmeadow model.

Calmeadow is a privately owned foundation that invests start-up funds in relatively small amounts to support the creation of small businesses. Loans are given to small circles of people, each of whom tries to ensure the survival of the others' businesses and the repayment of the loan. Calmeadow operates in some Aboriginal communities.

Participants compared the relationship between Calmeadow and Aboriginal people with their experiences with banks and government economic development programs. Participants said they often feel frustrated by poor bank relations when seeking loans, by the legal system and its complexities, and with committees and agencies that seem to create more problems than solutions.

The participants said that few Aboriginal people are able to take advantage of mainstream economic development programs. Such programs are aimed primarily at individuals rather than communities. As a result, they said, there is little community involvement, to tell government what businesses they thought would work or what was needed in their communities, and no control over the program.

Participants said Aboriginal urban people have economic strategies but lack the necessary capital or plan of action to develop new Aboriginal businesses in urban centres. They said they need to identify the types of businesses feasible for Aboriginal urban people. They also have to target sources of funding to support these businesses initially. They need to develop training and internship programs to produce business managers. In other words, participants said, they have to "get more aggressive" when it comes time to set up and run new Aboriginal-owned businesses in urban centres.

Some participants expressed fears about self-government because it might mean changes in economic development and federal funding policies.

Access to Employment

Participants said that government employment and job creation programs do not benefit many Aboriginal urban people. They said there is a tendency for one level of government to shuffle Aboriginal urban people to another level of government – from federal to provincial or municipal governments and vice versa. People working in federal employment offices do not seem to know about programs provided by other levels of government that might benefit Aboriginal applicants. The result, said participants, is a shuffling of Aboriginal urban people from one office to another.

The participants said there is a similar lack of co-ordination and information sharing about employment opportunities within the Aboriginal urban community. Aboriginal businesses or offices might have an opening but there is no co-ordinating office to advertise these jobs within the Aboriginal urban community. Similarly, there is no central bulletin board through which an unemployed Aboriginal person could market his or her skills. As one participant put it,

> Aboriginal people must take the initiative to market their own skills
> and should co-ordinate efforts within communities so that the right
> hand knows what the left hand is doing.

Participants also identified the lack of a central office that could approach non-Aboriginal businesses or employers in urban centres to encourage the hiring of Aboriginal people. They said existing Aboriginal organizations, friendship centres and Aboriginal businesses must market their people more effectively and take direct steps to change employers' attitudes about hiring Aboriginal people.

> Friendship centres can play an important role in the areas of employ-
> ment development and language training because they are status-
> blind. Employment programs should also be linked to women's shel-
> ters, emergency housing, parenting programs and literacy training.

Better marketing of Aboriginal people in the non-Aboriginal community is only part of the job, participants said. They said many Aboriginal people don't know how to look for a job. They might need help writing resumés or coaching in how to approach job interviews.

> Aboriginal people should be more aggressive about starting businesses, networking, and finding work through volunteer contacts. You don't find a job by looking in the newspaper – it's who you know. In general, Aboriginal people need to learn to market themselves.

Finally, participants said, there is the hurdle of racism and discrimination on the job. Many of these barriers to fair access to employment were supposed to be redressed under employment equity laws. However, the participants said employment equity legislation "has no teeth" and it allows employers to misuse and or refuse to comply with the law.

For example, participants said that Aboriginal people are kept in blue-collar or clerical ghettoes, while employers are allowed to claim success in achieving employment equity based on overall numbers. Employees are also denied opportunities for training or advancement. They are sometimes paid less than their non-Aboriginal counterparts in similar jobs. They are often the last hired and the first fired.

The participants said cross-cultural training might help, but they preferred that governments strengthen employment equity laws to ensure that Aboriginal urban people have equal opportunities for employment in urban centres.

Many of the participants had criticisms of the Pathways To Success Program sponsored by the Canada Employment and Immigration Commission. Some participants from Quebec said Pathways had made few contributions to job creation in that province because of language and cultural barriers. One participant said the majority of the people sitting on these boards are francophone, while the majority of Aboriginal people in Quebec speak English, so it has been especially difficult for them to find jobs.

Recommendations

Consistently, participants viewed Aboriginal urban people as a separate group from reserve-based or territorially-based Aboriginal people. As such, Aboriginal urban people need specific programs aimed at their needs and accountable to their populations.

In addition, throughout the workshops, but most notably in economics, participants recommended that some effort be made to address the issue of self-esteem in Aboriginal urban communities. The participants said that the economic situation in Aboriginal urban communities cannot be addressed as a narrow economic issue; poverty, joblessness and lack of economic opportunities are rooted in social conditions and cultural degradation. Both social and economic development must occur hand in hand before economic development can be successful, there must be efforts to improve the social and cultural well-being of Aboriginal urban people. The participants also offered the following recommendations:

- Economic development programs should be based on long-term funding and consistent criteria.
- Aboriginal control over program design, delivery and evaluation should be dominant features of economic development programs.
- Economic development initiatives and programs should be more accountable to the Aboriginal urban community.
- Training and human resource development should be integral parts of economic development policy and programs.
- Discrimination and systemic racism are sometimes barriers to sustainable development and, therefore, economic policy must address these issues.
- Joint ventures between Aboriginal economic initiatives and government, the private sector and other Aboriginal entrepreneurs and corporations should be promoted and enhanced.
- A successful economic development strategy must also include components dealing with cultural and social development issues.
- There must be stronger, more meaningful support for Aboriginal entrepreneurs, including management development, marketing training and initiatives aimed at providing easier access to capital.
- A public education campaign to address racism, negative stereotypes and the negative self-perception of Aboriginal people, which inhibits their participation in urban economies, should be initiated.

Governance

General Statements

A Commission member said the Commission needs to know "how self-government could apply to Aboriginal people in the city...in terms of hospital and school boards...and in terms of delivery." He also asked whether it is necessary for self-government to have a territory and urged participants to think in terms of services, not in terms of links to organizations. He also asked whether self-government can include Métis, and other Aboriginal groups or whether separate departments will be needed to deal with each type of status.

Of all of the workshops on Aboriginal urban issues, the topic of governance generated the most confusion and debate among delegates. Despite statements such as the one just quoted, some delegates wondered why there was a separate workshop on the topic of governance.

> It seems that the Commission decided to divide governance from services but there is a great deal of overlap among the four issue headings of economics, health, services and governance.

Issues such as racism had been identified as central problems in the lives of Aboriginal urban people in every area of discussion. These, contended some delegates, were the crucial issues that need to be addressed. Define the problems, delegates had been instructed, then suggest practical solutions. When it came to suggesting a practical form of Aboriginal urban governance, however, the discussion foundered on the thorny topic of jurisdiction.

> It is not clear who will have the power in Aboriginal urban communities, how that power will be institutionalized, or where the resources will come from.

However, the problems created or exacerbated by overlapping or non-existent federal, provincial and municipal jurisdiction affecting Aboriginal peoples, as another delegate explained, are anything but simple. For treaty or status Indians, for instance,

> Under the current system peoples rights are tied to the land. People who move off a reserve land base are all of a sudden floating... It is not a question of jurisdiction. It is a question of a vacuum. A participant said her identity changes if she moves, that it isn't tied to her, that it depends on where she lives.

For Métis and non-status Indians,

> Jurisdiction has been a stumbling block for the Métis ever since the BNA Act. S.24 of the BNA Act talks about "Indians, and Lands reserved for the Indians" and yet the Department of Health and Welfare says "you are not our responsibility, go see the province" and the province told him to "go see the feds."

Inuit in urban centres face similar problems. The rights of Inuit end at the settlement limits.

Participants saw the potential for further complications in their discussion of a third order of government as envisioned in constitutional negotiations. Aboriginal governments were not seen by all delegates as the answer to problems such as racism, high unemployment, poor housing or low education levels. Neither was the constitutional entrenchment of the inherent right to self-government perceived as ending jurisdictional conflicts. Problems may be aggravated by a lack of political development in urban areas and the multiplicity of jurisdictions.

For instance, the vast majority of delegates agreed that any form of Aboriginal urban governance had to be accountable and responsive to the people served – the Aboriginal urban population.

> There are different needs, different levels of services and different levels of functions. We have to have a certain flexibility of attitude.

> There is a need for a bottom-up, community-driven process. Don't take accountability away from the people.

> There is no process in urban areas... We need an urban-driven process to give people an equal voice.

Some delegates said an Aboriginal urban government had to safeguard and implement Aboriginal land rights, treaty rights and status rights even in urban areas. People felt frustration with a system that tells them once they leave the reserve they have no treaty rights.

> Urban residents must be able to access treaty rights. Treaty 6 and Treaty 7 cover social services, but Treaty 8 does not; therefore, social services must be covered by the provinces.

A man from The Pas, Manitoba, said he pays the same municipal taxes as non-Aboriginal people, but the town expects him to pay for his social services. Why, he wondered, can't services come from the same source?

Representation

Participants routinely identified jurisdictional problems in every area of discussion, whether it was economic development, health or services. These problems, they said, stem from the way federal legislation divides Aboriginal people into different categories with different rights. These same laws further divide a single Aboriginal group into several other categories, again with differing rights attached. For instance, these laws imposed different regimes on status or treaty Indians and on non-status or Bill C-31 Indians.

> We need to decide what Aboriginal people want in this country...particularly with regard to self-government. The word 'we' includes the Indians, the Inuit and the Métis. The latest expression is the inherent right to self-government. We want to control our own lives...whatever that might include and we want Indian workers and Métis workers deciding and administering for the Indian and Métis peoples.

These representational statements reflect the overwhelming sentiments of Aboriginal participants at the round table on urban issues. Participants asked, does 'we' mean Aboriginal urban people collectively or does it mean urban status people, urban treaty Indians, urban Métis, urban non-status Indians or urban Inuit peoples separately? The question of representation was debated and discussed but no single answer was unanimously accepted.

Furthermore, participants said, governments have established sometimes stark and ill-defined lines of jurisdiction over certain Aboriginal groups but excluded other groups. For example, the federal government has jurisdiction for First Nations people on-reserve but denies responsibility for status or treaty Indians off-reserve. The provincial government says urban status Indians are a federal responsibility, yet it applies its laws on reserves. Participants said these legal definitions, when combined with confusing and conflicting lines of jurisdiction, create a jurisdictional void when it comes to Aboriginal urban people.

At the same time, Aboriginal organizations claim to represent Aboriginal urban people but involve little accountability and almost no voice for Aboriginal urban people. For instance, many programs apply only to on-reserve status or Treaty Indians and are not extended to off-reserve Indians. Similarly, Métis and non-status groups receive funding for services in urban areas but deny that service to status or Treaty Indians. In other words, participants said, each Aboriginal organization practises its own form of discrimination with respect to the Aboriginal urban population.

As a result, participants said, many Aboriginal urban people fall through the cracks. They are counted in by provincial governments when it comes time to determine per capita funding, but they are denied services or cannot access services when it comes time to benefit from these resources. Some participants said this leaves Aboriginal urban populations in dependency and poverty – and powerless to change things.

One woman described going from Band Council to Chief to other agencies while seeking a college sponsorship. Leaving the reserve left her in limbo for sponsorship, she said. Until we stop discrimination against ourselves, how do we expect others to stop it?

Participants agreed that there was a tremendous amount of waste and duplication, inefficiency and a lack of co-ordination in the delivery of services. They said this was attributable to both an overlapping and an absence or denial of jurisdiction and mandates. Hence, the need for a status-blind approach to service delivery that would result in a more efficient, less wasteful and more humane system for delivering health and social services to an Aboriginal urban population.

However, a co-ordinated status-blind approach to service delivery also implies a status-blind approach to funding and administration. Many other participants felt this would come perilously close to undermining recognized rights of certain Aboriginal groups and the mandates of established Aboriginal political organizations. Some considered it a move that would further erode cultural and Aboriginal identities. A few said it would amount to nothing short of assimilation.

> We are governments. We have to have a government-to-government relation and be funded as such. These are the things our governments provide. These are the services that we provide when we sit down. That's the level that we need to get ourselves thinking at. That's the kind of pressure that you need to apply to your Aboriginal leadership. Because until that's done, nothing is going to change. We can talk about all these practical implementations and recommendations until we're blue in the face, but until we get recognition of who we are as a people, nothing is going to change.

To others, however, the establishment of a status-blind structure to oversee the delivery of services, and perhaps even the establishment of status-blind Aboriginal urban political organizations, were logical steps toward reversing some of the historical differences among the major Aboriginal groups. Some participants spoke strongly against extending the jurisdiction of territorial-based Aboriginal governments to include Aboriginal urban populations.

Some participants said that corruption exists in every government of every society and it would probably also exist in any new Aboriginal urban political organization as well. They said that whichever system Aboriginal urban people opt for, if they were given a choice, Aboriginal urban people had to have a representative voice.

Political organizations, whether they are territorially-based or uniquely urban, must be responsive and responsible to Aboriginal urban people. They said this might mean changing existing Aboriginal political organizations to include Aboriginal urban people. It might mean the establishment of new, strictly urban, Aboriginal organizations. But the arrangement had to be answerable to or controlled by Aboriginal urban people.

> I don't mind giving anybody power in this circle at all – but I expect accountability. Accountability has to be attached to that power. If there's no accountability, that power means nothing. And this is what is very scary in various areas because we tend to follow existing government structures. It gets back to our provincial or federal structure of patronage. And it's no secret that that exists in our own circle and it always will. But my key concern is accountability. If we've got accountability there, we've got a partial lid on that power.

Some participants said it boils down to a question of 'self-identification'. Aboriginal urban people should have the freedom to choose which group they belong to and, therefore, which organization would represent them politically. In this way, everybody could retain ties to their particular home community, retain their treaty or Aboriginal rights and strengthen their cultural identity. Aboriginal rights and identity would then be 'portable', maintained and not undermined.

In all the workshops held during the round table, this debate was repeated time and again without resolution. Participants said the distinctions between status or Treaty Indian, Bill C-31 (1985 amendments to the *Indian Act*) Indian, non-status Indian, Métis and Inuit are 'foreign' distinctions "that have been imposed upon us." They identified these differences as ultimately divisive or disruptive for Aboriginal people in urban centres. But they could neither leave these distinctions behind nor develop a means of getting beyond them.

One group, from Winnipeg, said it was in the process of establishing an "urban tribal council" to represent and serve urban status or Treaty Indians. Another group in the same city was trying to establish a status-blind Aboriginal urban administration to run a common services centre for all Aboriginal urban people. Others said there already exists such a status-blind urban organization in friendship centres. However, several participants pointed out that this organization is severely underfunded and is not permitted, by its own founding charter, to engage in the kinds of political activities they foresaw.

Even if participants could not agree on a mechanism, they did agree on a position most had reached even before the round table began.

> There is a need for a clear urban representative body that is heard by government.

Urban Structures

A majority of participants agreed on the need for status-blind service centres in major cities across Canada. The question of which existing Aboriginal organization would administer these centres was not resolved. However, participants did agree on certain points that might make the establishment of these service centres possible.

The institution would have to be established along principles that are Aboriginal in nature – it should not be merely a clone of non-Aboriginal institutions. There are few examples of such institutions at present, however.

There was agreement, however, that the service centres and their administration would have to be responsive to the needs and accountable to the Aboriginal urban population. Since the Aboriginal urban population is diverse, if not divided, participants proposed the creation of a services board with representation from the various groups within the Aboriginal urban population and possibly reserve and settlement Indian and Métis representation as well.

> The organization should provide a unified status blind voice and eliminate unnecessary duplication of services. It should be a political body representing both grassroots people and service organizations. Such a body would need real power in order to be effective. One working example, the United Native Nations in Vancouver, has served as a model for the Native Council of Canada. A similar model in Regina was relatively unsuccessful due to political disagreements.

Participants said the services board and service centres would need long-term funding in order to be effective. This would allow the establishment of various advisory boards made up of community members. These advisory boards would ensure that Aboriginal urban people had a voice in directing the service centres and providing for accountability.

Some participants said there need not be new funding; existing funding programs could be adapted and existing funds redirected. This would ensure that present services would not be interrupted.

Many participants saw an expanded role for friendship centres in establishing this structure of service delivery. Friendship centres are already status-blind and do much of the work already. Why can't they play a central role in guiding the establishment of these service centres, one participant wondered.

Some participants envisioned the creation of a 'super agency' for the Aboriginal urban population but others did not. They feared the quality of service would suffer if one agency tried to provide all of the services an Aboriginal urban population might require. As one participant said, "I'm against one-stop shopping when it comes to services. People who provide daycare may not know about the needs of the elderly or about street kids." She went on to explain that

> ...for several years, we've been trying to purchase the old CP railway station. The idea isn't to have one organization; it's to have several organizations housed in one building having social services, employment, medical services, daycare – everything you need, although it might not be one organization, we'd be housed in one centre.

Some participants suggested that these services and the service board would constitute a 'parallel municipal government' in urban centres. However, other participants took into account the number of Aboriginal urban people involved in various non-Aboriginal municipal activities. They sit on police boards, parole boards and school boards in some urban centres, for instance.

They said this approach should be encouraged and expanded to give Aboriginal urban people more say in civic administration and promote better co-ordination of services. They said there would be no danger of undermining the service centres proposed by participants. In fact, they said, having more Aboriginal people at city hall might help.

> More and more responsibility is falling down from the federal to the provincial and to the municipalities and that's why the municipalities were so interested in this round table. Because they're getting a lot of demands and they're making decisions about things that affect all of us, like transportation, and recreation and services. In what way are those kinds of decisions about planning going to be affected? How can Aboriginal people in the cities get onto positions to influence that planning, to get the information about what the needs are?

Participants also considered the educational issues. They said Aboriginal people could not expect to have the kinds of schools that now exist. There is room for alternative Aboriginal schools, but Aboriginal people need to be represented more on existing school boards in order to ensure the best education for their children.

The delegates decided to put these proposals forward with one proviso: whatever structure or structures might be negotiated with non-Aboriginal governments, the mechanisms had to be flexible. They emphasized that the Aboriginal urban population is diverse and includes a number of groups with a wide variety of concerns. When structures are designed, they must be flexible enough to allow these various groups to pursue their particular interests and find their own solutions.

Recommendations

The delegates in the governance workshops said their main concerns were the imposed divisions among groups of Aboriginal peoples. These divisions create jurisdictional buck passing. As a result, Aboriginal urban people in need of social services, education and job training, for example, routinely fall through the cracks.

They noted that rights derived from their home territories are cut off by the federal government once Aboriginal people go beyond their territorial boundaries and move into urban centres. The delegates said it was as if they suddenly became non-Aboriginal people in many instances. The delegates said their rights were portable and that, if necessary, someone should launch a court case to challenge denial of their rights by federal or provincial governments. They said governments are violating their constitutional rights, their Aboriginal and treaty rights and their freedom of movement rights, as guaranteed in the *Canadian Charter of Rights and Freedoms.*

Participants made several observations and recommendations, some of which address these concerns but most of which address the need to consolidate and co-ordinate status-blind services in urban areas. Some of the following recommendations are a result of intense discussion, while others are longstanding recommendations for reform that have never been implemented.

- The Royal Commission must identify and fund a research process to develop a service delivery model that will meet the needs of urban people.
- Jurisdictional options include the urban reserve and governance models in Winnipeg, Calgary, and Edmonton. The need for land, infrastructure and services must be addressed.
- A grassroots consultation process must take place around jurisdictional models. Aboriginal organizations must work together on roles and mandates, with no involvement of non-Aboriginal people except by invitation.
- The issue of portability of treaty rights must be addressed as soon as possible.
- Aboriginal representatives on boards and commissions must be accountable to Aboriginal urban people.
- Differences in Aboriginal identification do exist and must be considered in any negotiations around service delivery. But service providers, not politicians, should decide how services will be delivered.
- Each city needs a local council of elders and an ombudsman to ensure the delivery of quality services.
- The Royal Commission must support women's equality within the constitutional process. The Commission should also review Bill C-31, which still needs a great deal of work to remove sex discrimination.

Conclusion

Aboriginal participants in the round table identified the problems they face in urban centres across Canada. They described the programs they have devised to serve the needs of Aboriginal urban people. They isolated many of the specific conditions that hamper these efforts.

Participants described the social problems as a combination of ills: poverty, powerlessness, racism, joblessness, poor housing, family violence, abuse, AIDS, lack of child care, and low education and literacy levels. These problems are widespread and severe. Aboriginal urban people have developed programs aimed at alleviating these conditions and bettering the lives of Aboriginal urban people.

Participants connected many of these problems with cultural degradation and erosion: colonialism, assimilation, loss of language, loss of traditions, lack of traditional or cultural institutions and structures, loss of identity and low self-esteem.

In almost every case, participants explained, they have tried to combine the social services they provide to Aboriginal urban people with cultural components to deal with the effects of cultural erosion and loss of identity. Participants also emphasized that solutions to social problems in Aboriginal urban communities that fail to address the cultural, emotional and spiritual needs of Aboriginal people are merely band-aid solutions.

The structural problems, as many participants stated, are obvious. There is a general lack of funding and lack of support attributed in large measure to a disturbing ignorance on the part of all levels of government of the depth and the nature of the problems in Aboriginal urban communities. There is duplication of some services, insufficient co-ordination, and a total lack of other services. This problem can be addressed, participants said, only by creating central Aboriginal urban organizations that could streamline and create coherence where there is now underfunding, artificial divisions and confusion. Mostly, though, there is a jurisdictional void; all levels of government offload their responsibilities to Aboriginal urban people upon other levels of government. Participants felt that all governments, including Aboriginal governments, deny their obligations to Aboriginal urban people.

Legal definitions have been imposed on all Aboriginal people and have also been applied to Aboriginal urban people but without the rights these definitions imply. In most cases, territorial-based rights are not recognized beyond the boundaries of specific territories or extended into urban areas. First Nations vie with the other Aboriginal groups, Métis or Inuit, as well as with status-blind service delivery organizations, for access to funds. Participants also described internal racism; these divisions have led to further fragmentation of Aboriginal urban communities.

Although Aboriginal people of all groups condemn these divisions as ultimately self-defeating and plead for internal Aboriginal unity, the political divisions are deep. They stem from different legal definitions, different legal bases for rights, and different political aims.

Some Aboriginal urban people feel caught in the push and pull of competing Aboriginal organizations and powerful governments. They have no recognized political representation. They have no political voice. They are a fragmented, divided and still very transient population.

Yet, many have developed a new Aboriginal urban identity, separate and apart from the territorial-based Aboriginal identities. They expressed a wish to remain Aboriginal, to remain First Nations, Inuit or Métis, and to retain the rights derived from their legal status. They wish to assert these rights within the urban setting. Many have been born to the urban identity; others have become urban by choice or necessity.

Some want urban-based, Aboriginal political organizations to represent their concerns and apply their political will. In some cases, they feel the existing Aboriginal governments and organizations do not represent them.

Others, however, retain strong kinship, cultural, linguistic and political ties with their territorially-based counterparts. They wish to have these ties strengthened and reaffirmed. They too wish to have their rights applied in the urban setting. Their wish, however, is to see the territorial-based Aboriginal organizations such as band councils, Métis locals, tribal councils, provincial and national organizations extend their jurisdiction beyond the present boundaries to include Aboriginal urban populations.

People in every workshop addressed these questions. They said that what governments want is essentially irrelevant. These are questions of their own Aboriginal cultural and political identity. These were things that governments could no longer legislate as they had done with the *Indian Act*. They said it was something they would have to work out for themselves.

Participants said they would need to develop their own urban positions on these matters. It might mean urban community conferences and meetings. It might mean a process of self-identification and perhaps a realignment of urban organizations. They would need to be supported in these efforts and in the inevitable discussions with existing Aboriginal organizations and with non-Aboriginal governments. But ultimately, these decisions have to be made by urban Aboriginal people.

Issue Papers

Dan David*

AIDS

> A conservative estimate of the number of Aboriginal people who are HIV-positive and living in the city of Toronto is 50.
>
> Susan Beaver
> Two-Spirited People of the First Nations
> Toronto

 Many Aboriginal people are no different from other Canadians when it comes to AIDS. They believe AIDS can't or won't infect them. It's somebody else's disease, a 'gay disease', or they're somehow immune.

Yet AIDS is colour-blind. It does not discriminate by race, social class or income level. So far, more than 3,200 Canadians from all races, occupations and walks of life have been found to be HIV-positive, which means they have been infected by the virus that is thought to cause AIDS. About half these have died of AIDS or AIDS-related complications.

The U.S. Centres for Disease Control predicts that the first wave of AIDS has passed and that the second wave of HIV infection will be "in the poorer populations". George Poitras, of the Feather of Hope Aboriginal AIDS Prevention

---

* These background papers were prepared for the Round Table on Aboriginal Urban Issues by Dan David, Handsome Lake Productions. Opinions expressed in the papers are those of Mr. David and do not necessarily reflect the opinion or position of the Commission.

Society in Vancouver, considers this an ominous warning for Aboriginal people, who have been identified as a high-risk group.

The incidence of sexually transmitted diseases (STDs) is about three times higher in Aboriginal populations than in the rest of the population. There is a lack of adequate health care and sex education in Aboriginal communities. Substance abuse rates are higher, and this activity is often accompanied by sexual promiscuity. Teen pregnancy rates are also higher.

Aboriginal people are also highly transient, moving frequently between urban centres and Aboriginal communities. Needle exchange programs in Vancouver and Edmonton report that 40 per cent and 55 per cent of their clients respectively are Aboriginal people. Some Aboriginal people believe that AIDS could be just as destructive to Aboriginal populations as previous waves of diseases such as tuberculosis and smallpox and that public education is the best prevention. However, they face tremendous social and cultural barriers in getting the message out.

There is denial and fear of AIDS in Aboriginal communities, just as there is in the rest of Canadian society. AIDS prevention groups, such as Feather of Hope and Two-Spirited People of First Nations (Toronto), report that few Aboriginal people volunteer for AIDS testing or even inquire for information, for fear of being ostracized. Many Aboriginal people believe AIDS is a gay white man's disease. Aboriginal gay people and people living with AIDS in Aboriginal communities are often shunned, even by relatives. Sex, and therefore discussion about safe sex, is considered a private matter in many Aboriginal cultures.

There is also a long history of distrust of doctors and hospitals. The word 'hospital' in many Aboriginal languages translates literally as 'a place where people go to die'. In addition, a sense of fatalism among some Aboriginal people contributes to apathy about AIDS. "Why should I worry about AIDS," one Aboriginal man told a reporter. "If I don't get shot, stabbed or drink myself to death, I'll probably step off a curb and get hit by a truck."

Aboriginal people living on-reserve or in remote communities who discover they have AIDS also discover there is no place for them to live or receive treatment in their communities. The harsh attitudes of their neighbours usually drive them out of their communities and into the cities. Once in the city, they face another set of prejudices and problems.

Aboriginal people with AIDS do not usually enter mainstream AIDS centres or hospices because they feel isolated and alone as a result of language and cultural differences. There are few Aboriginal AIDS workers in these centres, nor are they often sought. The impression seems to be that Aboriginal people are already adequately served somehow and somewhere else.

Substance Abuse

Herb (not his real name) says he arrived in Winnipeg from his reserve in north-ern Ontario ten years ago with a suitcase full of "hatred, anger and resentment. I mean I was really confused. I graduated from university but I couldn't find a job so I went back home because it was cheaper to live there."

He says he drank a lot back on "the rez" because there wasn't much else to do. "It seemed like the only time we had any fun was when we were drinking and acting crazy, you know?" He expected things to be different, more exciting, bet-ter, in the city.

"But after a while," he says, "it got pretty boring, just another kind of boring. No job. No money. No friends – except your drinking buddies. No services to help you. Lots of racism. After a while, your whole world revolves around your drinking buddies and the booze."

That's how Herb says he wound up on skid row. He became a drooling, stum-bling, sleep-in-the-park bums that people stared at. "You don't even care," he says now. "The only thing you cared about was that next bottle. You just have no self-respect."

During periods of sobriety, Herb would move from city to city, swearing he'd stay off the booze each time. Each time, he'd feel he had to move because he'd fall off the wagon and would quit his job or be fired.

"I had an education, a degree in education. I was a teacher. I guess I knew I was screwed up so I didn't try to teach. I worked in the government instead." He still drank, though, "to fit in". The only difference, he says, was that "now I was better dressed and I had money. But I was still a drunk."

Herb's story is not unusual. In 1985, the National Association of Friendship Centres (NAFC) released a study of substance abuse in urban centres based on a survey of 84 friendship centres nationwide. It reported that

> Very often, the clients come from the reserve environment into the city with hope of finding employment, but far too often because of their low education background and unskilled with little or no work experience, they become discouraged at finding any employment. In addition, they also do not have the family or community support in the city as they normally would back in the Indian community. So they go back into the trappings of the bottle for acceptance, confi-dence and courage.

The study found that statistical information about the actual or estimated extent of substance abuse by Aboriginal people in urban centres is "virtually non-exis-tent". Most of the clients of friendship centres, one of the few social agencies serving urban Aboriginal peoples, were seeking "other basic assistance (employment, housing, education)" and not specific help for substance abuse. The report tied the lack of these basic necessities with "increased use/abuse of alcohol, drugs and solvents."

Although the report did not provide estimates of the extent of the problem, it did find that "substance abuse is prevalent among Native people in urban communities...among all age and target groups with alcohol being the primary substance." It also included figures gathered by Aboriginal court workers in the Northwest Territories, Yukon and Quebec, which showed "that between 80 per cent and 95 per cent of their clients have substance abuse problems."

Thirty-eight of the 56 friendship centres reported that children in their communities were drinking alcohol or sniffing glue, gasoline, and other solvents. They did so "after school, during school recess, on the street, in parks, in their homes" or when their parents were out drinking and even "sometimes with the family."

One centre reported the case of "a father who liked seeing kids get high, gave a 5-year old girl a can of PAM to sniff, and it coated her lungs – she suffocated."

Nearly all the centres reported similar horrific stories about substance abusers in older age groups, both men and women, chronic and casual abusers. The NAFC study found the negative effects to include "suicides, homicides, accidental deaths", a high incidence of fetal alcohol syndrome births, physical and sexual problems, physical, sexual and child abuse, and joblessness.

As in so many other areas, the study by the NAFC found gaps in the policies of the federal and provincial governments when it came to combating Aboriginal substance abuse in urban areas. NNDAP, a federal Indian substance abuse program administered by Health and Welfare, was perceived by provincial governments as a federal commitment to combat Aboriginal substance abuse and to include Indian, Métis and Inuit, on-reserve or in the cities. However, NNDAP is restricted to status Indians living on-reserve.

None of the provincial/territorial governments has a specific mandate to combat substance abuse among Aboriginal people, the NAFC study reported. The NAFC found that although provincial governments sympathized and understood the tremendous problems caused by substance abuse in urban Aboriginal communities, its "services to Native persons were incorporated into the overall mandate."

Child Welfare

> It would be reassuring if blame could be laid to any single part of the system. The appalling reality is that everyone involved believed they were doing their best and stood firm in their belief that the system was working well. Some administrators took the ostrich approach to child welfare problems – they just did not exist. The miracle is that there were not more children lost in this system run by so many well-intentioned people. The road to hell was paved with good intentions, and the child welfare system was the paving contractor.
>
> Judge Edwin Kimelman
> *No Quiet Place* (1982)

With those words in a inquiry report a mere ten years ago, Edwin Kimelman, Chief Judge of the Family Division of Manitoba's Provincial Court, condemned the almost routine practice of the province's child welfare authorities of taking Aboriginal children into custody. "No one fully comprehended that 25 per cent of all children placed for adoption were placed outside of Manitoba," Kimelman wrote. "No one fully comprehended that virtually all those children were of Native descent. No one comprehended that Manitoba stood alone amongst all provinces in this abysmal practice."

Kimelman pulled no punches in his report, *No Quiet Place*. "Even one Native child removed from his family and his culture constitutes cultural genocide," he wrote. Kimelman found the apprehension and removal of Aboriginal children from their families, their communities and their cultures by child welfare agencies was "routine". The practice of out-of-province adoptions only compounded the outrage.

All parties were at fault, he continued – federal and provincial governments that failed to resolve jurisdictional disputes for the care of Aboriginal children, child welfare directors who were unaccountable to their Aboriginal clientele, "the child care agencies, both public and private, who failed to examine the results of their policies and practices and who failed to keep accurate statistical data; the Native organizations who remained too silent, too long, before demanding control of their children."

Kimelman's report was a stinging rebuke of child welfare practices when applied to Aboriginal people. It referred repeatedly to cultural misconceptions held by child care workers about Aboriginal people and the way they raised their children. "Cultural bias in the child welfare system is practised at every level from the social worker who works directly with the family, through the lawyers who represent the various parties in a custody case, to the judges who make the final disposition in the case."

Kimelman recommended that the definition of what was in the "best interests" of Aboriginal children must include "the child's cultural and linguistic heritage"; that Aboriginal child care agencies should be established to care for Aboriginal children; that these agencies should not be restricted only to reserve boundaries but must also be responsible for the children of their members living in urban areas. He also recommended that the provincial government establish adoption subsidies to encourage potential Aboriginal foster parents.

Eight years later, the Manitoba Aboriginal Justice Inquiry concurred with Judge Kimelman in almost every respect. In the intervening years, however, the Inquiry found both federal and provincial governments still turning their backs on urban Aboriginal people; Aboriginal child welfare agencies still restricted to reserves; no Métis-run child care agencies; no subsidies to encourage Aboriginal foster parents; and an unacceptably high degree of apprehension and removal of Aboriginal children from their families and their cultures. The Inquiry did find, however, that non-Aboriginal child care agencies had begun to hire more Aboriginal social workers.

Culture

> Until we realize that [Aboriginal people] are not simply 'primitive versions of us' but a people with a highly developed, formal, complex and wholly foreign set of cultural imperatives, we will continue to misinterpret their acts, misperceive their problems, and then impose mistaken and potentially harmful 'remedies'.
>
> Rupert Ross
> *Dancing With A Ghost* (1992)

In 1982, Rosemarie Kuptana, now president of the Inuit Tapirisat of Canada, compared the effects of the wholesale introduction of non-Inuit culture into her people's communities to the destructive power of a neutron bomb. She could as easily have been describing the effects of assimilation and its impact on Aboriginal cultures:

> This is the bomb that kills the people but leaves the building standing...that destroys the soul of a people but leaves the shell of a people walking around. The pressure, especially on our children, to join the invading culture and language...is explosively powerful.

The damage to Aboriginal cultures from 150 years of assimilation has been acute. In 1984, a Canadian ethnologist estimated that only three of the fifty-three Aboriginal languages spoken in Canada had an excellent chance of surviving to the year 2000. "Our language," one Mohawk elder told a meeting on

Aboriginal languages a few years ago, "is the key to our culture...and our languages are dying."

Another elder explained the interrelationship between Aboriginal languages and cultures in this way:

> Our native language embodies a value system about how we ought to live and relate to each other...it gives a name to relations among kin, to roles and responsibilities among family members, to ties with the broader clan group... There are no English words for these relationships because your social and family life [are] different from ours. Now if you destroy our language, you not only break down these relationships, but you also destroy other aspects of our Indian way of life and culture, especially those that describe man's connection with nature, the Great Spirit and the order of things. Without our language we will cease to exist as a separate people.

Aboriginal cultural values, at a fundamental level, reflect a very different world view from that of European-Canadians. These world views are the basis for vastly different philosophies, values and practices. Each is the basis for differing customs, manners and what makes proper behaviours.

In the Judeo-Christian tradition, people are instructed to "have dominion" over "the fish in the sea, the birds of heaven, and every living thing that moves upon the earth." Human beings are considered supreme. In many Aboriginal philosophies, by contrast, "Humankind...[is] the most dependent and least necessary of all the orders." In other words, human beings are only one part of an intricate web of interdependent life.

The traditional cultural and social values of many Aboriginal people reflect these different concepts of acceptable behaviour. For instance, Ojibway, or Anishnabe, ceremonies instill values of wisdom, love, respect, bravery, honesty, humility and truth. "A study of the psychological and behavioural patterns of the Sioux identifies several central values for the Dakota people," reported the Aboriginal Justice Inquiry in Manitoba, which went on to elaborate on these values. "Conformity with the group and harmony within it; concentration on the present; ability to make personal decisions; reluctance to show emotions; reverence for nature even while using it; and constant awareness of God."

Other studies reveal that Aboriginal cultures embody similar values, such as ethics of non-interference, respect for individual freedom, co-operation and sharing. "While such cultural differences...have been noticed and remarked upon by various non-Aboriginal writers for hundreds of years," noted the Aboriginal Justice Inquiry, "few people have tried to explore and explain these differences in terms understandable to the general population. Instead, these differences have been explained away in terms of handy stereotypes and vague generalizations."

Dr. Clare Brant is the only clinical psychologist in Canada who is also an Aboriginal person, a Mohawk. He has studied and written about the cultural differences of Aboriginal peoples and what he calls "Aboriginal ethics and rules of behaviour". As he explains, these "ethics" grew out of the need for close-knit Aboriginal families, extended families, clans, tribes or nations of people to maintain harmony and ensure the survival of the group. Brant says these ethics of behaviour are most noticeable when contrasted with the 'normal' behaviour of non-Aboriginal Canadians.

Brant outlines four major Aboriginal ethics of behaviour: non-interference, non-competitiveness, emotional restraint, and sharing. These are complement-ed by four other rules: a different concept of time, the expression of gratitude and approval, social protocols, and the teaching and rearing of children. Brant – and many other sociologists – say Aboriginal people act differently because they follow different cultural rules of behaviour.

> When Aboriginal people refuse to follow the exhortations of our rules, we judge them as inefficient in rule-obedience or, worse, rule-less. In our ignorance, we have failed to admit the possibility that there might be rules other than ours to which they regularly display allegiance, an allegiance all the more striking because it is exercised in defiance of our insistent pressures to the contrary.

In the past, Aboriginal people have been denied the right to practise their religions and their ceremonies. Their cultures and philosophies have been demeaned and denigrated by non-Aboriginal people. As a consequence, many Aboriginal people have been reduced to a "shell of a people walking around", with diminished self-esteem.

"What has been suppressed by laws and other religions in the past are these traditional mechanisms by which Aboriginal people have dealt with personal problems and pressures," concluded the Manitoba Aboriginal Justice Inquiry. "Many of these ceremonies were outlawed by governments until very recently. These ceremonies are still dismissed or debased by some people, even today. The disruption of Aboriginal societies, for the most part, has not interfered greatly with such rules of behaviour, but it has interfered greatly with the means by which Aboriginal people maintained personal balance and well-being."

Daycare

June is a single Aboriginal mother with three children under the age of ten years living in Regina. She fits the Statistics Canada profile of off-reserve Aboriginal women: more numerous than Aboriginal men; with larger families; in poorer housing; having fewer opportunities; more dependent on social assistance; and more likely to enrol in post-secondary training programs. She is also the person most likely to benefit from daycare and much more likely not to have it or to use it.

However, June is lucky. She lives in Regina. The Native Council of Canada (NCC), the organization representing Métis and non-status Indians, estimates that June is one of 40,000 Aboriginal people living in the city. The NCC reports there are 5,720 daycare spaces in Regina and that nearly 75 per cent of these spaces are filled with Aboriginal children, including two of June's children. June's youngest child stays with her mother while she takes a secretarial course during the day.

June's situation is more than lucky – it is exceptional. The NCC survey of urban daycare found most Aboriginal people didn't have access to daycare – there were few if any services available for them – or they couldn't afford it even if it were available.

In the province of Quebec, for instance, the NCC found 6,480 daycare spaces. Yet only 24 Aboriginal children were enroled in daycare. The NCC found that language was a problem for some but most Aboriginal people did not know about daycare service or did not consider daycare an option.

In Winnipeg, with a population of 41,000 Aboriginal people, nearly half of all Aboriginal single-parent households have children under the age of 18. Twenty per cent of the Aboriginal single parents are under the age of 25, yet only a small percentage of Aboriginal children are enroled in daycare.

A study in Ontario found that although "urban Native respondents are active users of many human service agencies... half of the agency directors and service staff said that Native respondents were under-utilizing agency resources." The report went on to say that "One type of community resource that may not be used by Aboriginal people, where it is in existence, is the daycare centre. Nearly all questionnaires returned from daycare centres in the Task Force resource assessment study indicated no use by Native respondents."

The NCC study pointed to a lack of Aboriginal daycare facilities across the country. In British Columbia, with an off-reserve population estimated by the NCC at 60,000, only one Aboriginal daycare centre was found. In most urban areas, the NCC reports that Aboriginal single parents have "to compete with the general population for limited child care." In addition, few Aboriginal daycare workers are employed by non-Aboriginal daycare facilities.

The NCC study, entitled *The Circle of Care*, identified several areas of concern. First, it found a lack of culturally appropriate daycare facilities. Aboriginal parents, it found, needed to be assured that daycare would "not become another attempt to assimilate Native Peoples." The lack of Aboriginal daycare workers reinforced these fears.

Second, the NCC found confusion about the daycare system. For instance, who runs and regulates daycare? Was Aboriginal daycare accountable to Aboriginal people or to provincial rules and regulations? Third, who would pay for daycare services for Aboriginal people? The NCC found many of the parents surveyed were confused by the difference between private and public daycare, federal/provincial questions of jurisdiction and their role in determining guidelines.

The NCC study indicated that daycare was neither universal nor accessible to most Aboriginal parents. Aboriginal daycare in most urban areas was virtually non-existent. Culturally appropriate daycare, which would instil Aboriginal cultural values and allow Aboriginal children to hear their own language and see similar faces, was also virtually non-existent. However, the NCC also found that Aboriginal people in some urban areas are beginning to discover daycare as a means to allow them to improve their lives and further their education.

Employment/Business

The good news is that Aboriginal people living in urban areas are participating in the labour force in rates equal to other Canadians (65 per cent and 67 per cent respectively). The bad news is that urban Aboriginal people are twice as likely as their non-Aboriginal neighbours to be unemployed. The unemployment rate for Aboriginal people in urban areas is 21 per cent, compared to about 10 per cent for other Canadians in urban areas.

The problems aren't simple. Aboriginal people face discrimination in hiring and employment. They earn about one-third less in wages. They are less likely to hold down full-time, year-round jobs. They are much more likely to be employed in manual trades such as construction than in white collar jobs as professionals, administrators, managers or clerks.

However, the major impediment to increased Aboriginal participation in the labour force continues to be lower education levels and a lack of marketable skills. Figures from the Department of Indian Affairs and Northern Development show that "while significant improvements have been made in the educational achievements of Aboriginal people, much remains to be accomplished before they enjoy equitable access to the labour market and same standard of living that other Canadians are accustomed to."

The reason is simple. There just aren't enough jobs for the Aboriginal people entering the work force. "The dramatic improvements in educational achievements will be undermined if a young and more educated work force cannot find meaningful and rewarding work," warns the same Indian Affairs survey.

Since 1989, the federal government has tried to co-ordinate Aboriginal economic development in both on-reserve and urban areas through the Canadian Aboriginal Economic Development Strategy (CAEDS). CAEDS is administered through three federal departments, Industry, Science and Technology (ISTC), Indian and Northern Affairs Canada (INAC), and Employment and Immigration Canada. It has a national board with both Aboriginal and non-Aboriginal directors.

The budget for CAEDS, according to the chairperson, "has no pre-determined lifespan, although a total of $873.7 million ($399 million to ISTC and $474.7 million to INAC) was allocated for delivery of programs during the first five years." There is an additional $200 million a year administered through the Pathways to Success Program by Employment and Immigration Canada.

CAEDS was set up to encourage Aboriginal individuals, businesses and organizations to develop their own business and management skills, organize and set up businesses and lending institutions, and help secure loans. It is accessible to all Aboriginal people: status and non-status Indians, Métis and Inuit.

To date, CAEDS has invested $86 million jointly with other investors, Aboriginal and non-Aboriginal, for a total of $267 million. It has contributed $38 million to support loans to Aboriginal business. It has also spent $4.6 million to help Aboriginal business people prepare research and present their plans. This amounts to $129 million, or an average of $43 million a year, during the past three years.

Some critics says this isn't nearly enough to make a dent in the unemployment rates of Aboriginal people. They say that the lion's share of the CAEDS support goes to reserves and not enough goes to urban areas, to women, or to Métis. Others warn that without a boost to retraining and new skills development, the jobs may be created but there won't be enough trained and qualified people to fill the positions.

The final word goes to Ken Thomas, who chairs the national board of CAEDS. He says that although "the business development concerns of Aboriginal people have been partially addressed over the past few years...[CAEDS] was never intended to be the total answer."

Education

> In 1950...someone convinced us to let some children go to the residential school, and we sent ten students out. Maybe they weren't looked after, or maybe they could not get used to the environment, but anyway, they only ever sent back one of them, and nobody really knows what happened to the rest of them.
>
> Chief Saul Fiddler, Sandy Lake
> Quoted in the Report of the Royal Commission
> on the Northern Environment (1978)

Aboriginal people have always recognized education as the key to their own survival and co-existence with other peoples. Children absorbed their own languages, laws and values at their parents' side. Sometimes they learned the languages and laws of other peoples as well. They learned their own people's medicines, industries and technologies. They learned to provide for their families and ensure the security of their people.

Education was seen as a community responsibility, with parents sharing teaching duties with the extended family and the community. The elders of a community played a major role. They taught the children by example rather than through formal instruction or by rote. Through them, children learned; education was continuous and essential to their personal growth and to the welfare of the nation.

During the past 100 years, however, Aboriginal peoples' perception of education has changed. As European society became dominant, parents and elders were seen as disruptive influences to the 'proper' education of young Aboriginal children and their eventual assimilation into Euro-Canadian society. Responsibility for educating Aboriginal children was taken away from the parents and assumed by the federal government.

"The education provided to Indians by the Government of Canada...has been an important element of an overall policy of assimilation," wrote Diane Longboat in a research paper for the Assembly of First Nations. "It has been a means of seeking to...modify the values of the Indian nations through those who are the weakest and can offer the least resistance...the children. Education has worked with the long-term objective of weakening Indian nations through causing the children to lose sight of their identities, history and spiritual knowledge."

The results of low education standards, the denigration and denial of their Aboriginal cultures and languages, and the sometimes brutal experiences of students in federal residential schools contributed to a growing distrust of education. There were legislative sanctions too. Aboriginal students who attained a certain level of education were automatically stripped of their rights.

By 1966, a federal report summed up the result: "The atmosphere of the school, the routines, the rewards, and the expectations provide a critically different experience for the Indian child than for the non-Indian. Discontinuity of socialization, repeated failure, discrimination and lack of significance of the educational process in the life of the Indian child result in diminishing motivation, increased negativism."

Formal education was used to separate the Aboriginal child from his family and people. However, the educated Aboriginal child was still not accepted by white society. Finding few positive purposes in education, the Aboriginal child often chose to drop out rather than face the lonely prospect of straddling two worlds and fitting in neither.

The federal government has since returned control of most federal schools in Aboriginal communities back to Aboriginal parents. The results have been dramatic. In 1965, the percentage of Indian children who were dropping out before graduating high school was about 97 per cent. The latest figures available put the present drop-out rate at about 59 per cent, still far above the Canadian average of 25 to 30 per cent, but a significant improvement from thirty years ago. There are twice as many Aboriginal people staying in and graduating from high school today as there were ten years ago.

The enrolment of First Nations people in university and post-secondary institutions has increased from 60 in 1960 to more than 18,000. Some estimate the total number of Aboriginal people in post-secondary education this year at 40,000.

Despite improvements in Aboriginal-run schools, there has been little understanding of similar problems and disadvantages facing Aboriginal students in urban areas. A study of urban schools in Saskatchewan six years ago found that 90 per cent of Aboriginal students did not graduate from high school. Despite efforts to make the school materials "more relevant" to Aboriginal people, the drop-out figures have not improved.

In many urban schools, Aboriginal students still face alienating and irrelevant text materials and prejudice from non-Aboriginal students. Aboriginal parents continue to have little say in the education of their children. The drop-out rate for Aboriginal students in Regina has remained the same for the past ten years and is still about 90 per cent. Regina is not exceptional in this regard.

Governance

Aboriginal self-government is the recognition by Canadians that Aboriginal peoples have a fundamental right to determine their own lives through their own institutions within their own cultures, communities and lands. What does this mean, however, for Aboriginal people living in the cities?

According to figures from the federal government, about three-fourths (73 per cent) of all Aboriginal people live outside of reserves. "More specifically, there are approximately five hundred and fifty-two thousand persons of Aboriginal origin" out of a total population of 711,000 living off-reserve.

Although Ontario had the largest number of Aboriginal people living off-reserve or in urban areas, "they are *proportionately* more numerous in the western part of Canada." In all, people living off-reserve make up about two per cent of the total Canadian population.

Unfortunately, another department has another set of figures. These 'official' estimates are disputed by Aboriginal organizations, which place the urban Aboriginal population closer to 50 per cent, or half the total Aboriginal population. Whatever the actual figure, there is no denying there are significant numbers of Aboriginal people living in Canada's major cities.

They are not well served. Jurisdictional wrangling between the federal and provincial governments is the main culprit. Neither level of government is anxious to take responsibility. Social service programs with unclear mandates are hampered by unstable or inadequate funding, and many Aboriginal people fall through the cracks of government programs.

Aboriginal political organizations, most of which keep offices in urban centres, have been unwilling or unable to pick up the slack. For instance, status Indian and Inuit groups have been restricted by law or by policy to their constituencies on-reserve or in the home communities. Métis and non-status Indian groups claim to represent off-reserve or urban Aboriginal populations but in fact represent only a portion of these people.

The result is that urban Aboriginal populations have not had effective or accountable political representation. They are claimed by many groups, but the urban Aboriginal population remains nebulous, transitory and fragmented. This has allowed their needs and concerns to be easily overlooked or ignored.

Until recently, government services aimed at urban Aboriginal people concentrated on integrating them into the general population. However, friendship centres – which are among the few urban Aboriginal service agencies – view their role as countering this push toward cultural assimilation and shouldering more responsibility for the welfare of the urban Aboriginal population.

Despite the presence of friendship centres in many urban centres, urban Aboriginal people continue to lack political representation and organization. While some would like to see friendship centres become a political organization representing urban Aboriginal people, the strong loyalties of many Aboriginal people to their own communities and cultural groups make it unlikely. In fact, any sort of co-operative urban Aboriginal movement has been hamstrung by scarce resources, fragmented populations, unclear mandates, and a lack of Aboriginal, federal or provincial encouragement and support.

Some early suggestions that cities create well-designed, self-governing, Aboriginal residential communities within cities. The idea was that these communities would develop their own institutions and run their own services. This idea was contemplated during the 1970s in Winnipeg. However, it sounded too much like an Aboriginal ghetto to some people. Also, Aboriginal people found out the city would retain all real decision-making power. The plan was shelved.

Constitutional entrenchment of Aboriginal self-government might make similar schemes unlikely, although not impossible, in the future. With recognition of Aboriginal self-government, Aboriginal people would likely demand decision-making power over such a project. Lines of jurisdiction would have to be negotiated and agreed upon. However, an entirely new relationship would have to be worked out.

There are other models. Some studies suggest that certain urban Aboriginal professionals form societies to "represent the interests of individual Natives in their dealings with institutions in the larger Canadian society." They would play roles similar to those of non-governmental professional societies in some Commonwealth countries. They could not represent urban Aboriginal people politically but they could lobby for change and improvement.

Others suggest that urban Aboriginal people organize into "communities of interest" whose "territory would be cultural rather than geographical." For example, this community within a community might assume jurisdiction over a growing number of areas such as education, child welfare and health care. There has been some development in this area, with the Native Centre of Toronto establishing the Anishnabe Health Centre. It also has plans to expand into other areas as well.

There are also 'extra-territorial' models. The idea is that citizens of an Aboriginal nation retain benefits and obligations even if they move to the city. This model recognizes the strong cultural and family ties that many urban Aboriginal people have with their home territories. There would be some problems with status Indians, who might be excluded from decision making on a reserve. As a minority, their concerns might be given a low priority.

However, there are some working examples. The Canada-Manitoba-Indian Child Welfare Agreement allows regional Aboriginal child welfare agencies to assume responsibility for the children of status Indian band members beyond the borders of the reserve. Also, status Indians seeking post-secondary education are routinely served by educational counsellors in urban centres employed by their bands.

There are other examples. However, all of these models assume the inevitable handing over of responsibility to Aboriginal peoples for programs and services in urban areas to some extent.

Health

"It's very difficult to say anything positive about urban Aboriginal health," said Anne Bird of the Indian Health Care Commission which serves status Indians in Edmonton. "We've all known what the problems have been for a long time," she says. "Nothing is ever done about it."

"It" is the constant dispute between the federal, provincial and municipal governments over responsibility for providing health care to Aboriginal people living in urban centres. None want the responsibility. As a result, to avoid red tape and shuffling back and forth, Bird says, many Aboriginal patients wait "until there's a crisis and then they go to the emergency ward in a hospital."

Bird argues that Medical Services Branch of the Department of Health & Welfare accepts responsibility for the health care of Treaty Indians off-reserve "but only on paper and not in reality." Indians leave the reserves expecting to receive a similar level of health care when they arrive in the city. "But once you leave the reserve, you stop being a treaty Indian. You stop being entitled to the same health care you got on the reserve."

The constant jurisdictional buck passing is the number one problem in Bird's view. Insensitivity and lack of understanding of Aboriginal people and their cultures rates a close second. "A lot of people, including a lot of doctors and nurses, are insensitive to Indians."

Inaccessibility and unfamiliarity are two other major problems Bird identifies. "Many people just don't know what services are available or what kind of help they can get. Sometimes, the service is there but they just can't get to it. I know the same problems exist with Métis and non-status Indians in this city. It's frustrating."

There are about 27,000 Aboriginal people in Edmonton. The Aboriginal population in Toronto is estimated to be near 80,000. The same problems exist in

Toronto, says Shirley Morrison, health promotion co-ordinator with the Anishnabe Health Centre. Aboriginal people there decided they had to deliver their own health care, in their own way, to their own people. With the support of the provincial Ministry of Health, the Anishnabe Health Centre opened its doors two years ago.

According to Morrison it was a case of all levels of government, especially the provincial and municipal governments, recognizing a tragic situation and deciding something had to be done. "The Ministry of Health and the City of Toronto have been very supportive. They realized they couldn't reach the people who really needed help," she says.

When the Anishnabe Health Centre opened in downtown Toronto, Shirley Morrison says the staff were surprised by the Aboriginal people who showed up at the door. They expected to see a lot of unemployed Aboriginal people, a lot of women who were single parents, a lot of people living in substandard housing and surviving on welfare. This was, after all, the profile of the Aboriginal people going to other clinics.

However, Morrison says, "We were struck by the huge number of Aboriginal street people who walked in the door. So many were homeless. We also found it unusual that for every two men there was one woman. It's usually reversed, with more women accessing health care than men."

The Anishnabe Health Centre is reaching people who, for whatever reasons, could not or would not visit a non-Aboriginal health facility. Morrison believes a large part of the reason is that "We're all Aboriginal people here, except for a couple of the doctors. We know what they've been through. We know where they come from. We care about them."

"Anishnabe Health opened with the promise of reaching Aboriginal people who couldn't or wouldn't go to the usual clinics and facilities. We're different. We're all Aboriginal...and, obviously, these people feel comfortable coming here. We know their problems."

"Many of these problems can be traced back to the residential schools. Many of the people we see were physically or sexually abused there or maybe their parents were. We're seeing a lot of people who come from dysfunctional families. There's a lot of family violence, physical and sexual abuse. Many use alcohol and substances, drugs, to deaden the pain. Many of their health problems can be traced to or are made worse by mental health problems."

The Anishnabe Health Centre has tried to change the system to fit the culture, says Morrison, admitting that it doesn't solve all the problems. "Jurisdictional disputes cause problems." However, she says, "We've been most successful because we adopt a traditional approach to healing, a more holistic approach. They feel comfortable coming here. They'd wait for an emergency to go some-place else."

Homelessness

It's funny you should bring up that spot. A group of guys used to hang around the hot air vent on the corner of the street, especially when it got really cold. It got pretty famous. Then some city work crews went there and plugged up the vent. Or at least they tried to plug it up, to drive the guys off the street and out of sight. The city health and social services departments understood the problem but the message hasn't reached the city works department yet.

Shirley Morrison
Anishnabe Health Centre,
Toronto

When Shirley Morrison started working at the Anishnabe Health Centre she says she didn't understand the different forces at work against the homeless, especially the Aboriginal homeless. After two years on the job, she feels she's begun to understand the enormous scope of the problems.

Everybody treats the issue as if it can be compartmentalized into easily dealt with areas. The housing department treats it as a problem in housing. The health department treats it as a health problem. The social services department treats it as a social service problem. But homelessness isn't an easy issue. It's a problem for all of these depart-ments, including the city works department, all at the same time, and they have to realize that.

Morrison estimates the number of Aboriginal homeless people in Toronto to be "between 5,000 and 10,000 people." She knows this is an enormous number of people and an enormous problem in the city of Toronto. As a health care work-er, she feels concerned about the homeless as a health care issue. However, she also knows "their health is affected by their lack of a decent place to live, by their unemployment, by their inability to access social services and by their own unwillingness to seek help."

For instance, Morrison explains, "a lot of the guys don't go to the non-Aboriginal shelters in the city. They know there's a lot of stealing, a lot of fights and beatings there. They also know there aren't enough places, and they feel discriminated against when they go there. They'll access a hostel if they can but there aren't enough of them. So they stay out on the street."

Similar problems, on a lesser scale, exist in cities across Canada. In Montreal, the Native Friendship Centre conducted a survey of some of the homeless people in that city. Here is one profile:

> Andrea first came to Montreal with the aid of Health and Welfare Canada for treatment of a hearing problem. At this time, she began hanging out in bars frequented by other Inuit. Andrea missed two flights home and finally had to pay for her own flight back to Cape Dorset. After she returned home, she decided to leave and return to Montreal [because of family problems].

> Andrea has been on the streets of Montreal for the last three years. Sometimes her father sends her money. Mostly, she solicits. She admitted she has six regular customers a week and charges them anywhere from $30 to $300 a trick. When she works, she works four days a week and finds her customers in bars and occasionally on the streets.

> Systematic abuse is part and parcel of Andrea's life.

Andrea's story is all too familiar to the people who conducted the survey in Montreal. They found that while many Aboriginal people moved to the city in search of an education or jobs, many others fled their communities escaping physical, emotional and sexual abuse, extreme poverty and despair. However, they escaped only to encounter similar conditions in the city.

> Joanne left home at the age of 18 and has gone back occasionally for short visits, stating she does not like the reserve. She was introduced to street soliciting by a white man who picked her up at the bus terminal when she first came to Montreal. She has been on the street for six years.

> Systematic abuse is also a part of Joanne's life. She stated that she's been verbally abused by prostitutes as well as physically abused by customers and by her pimp.

> Joanne told us she would like to get rid of her pimp and "work at something different". She says she "would like to be a woman like any other".

"It's the same in every city," says Anne Bird, who works with the Indian Health Care Commission. "It's the same in Vancouver, or Winnipeg or Regina. People leave their reserves and come into the cities thinking things will be better. But they're not. There's no housing, no social workers and they can't access health care. And nobody tells them before they come."

Aboriginal housing programs, like Kikinew Housing in Vancouver, Inuit Housing in Ottawa, and the Aboriginal Women's Shelter in Montreal, try to provide shelter or housing. Aboriginal health care workers, like those at the Anishnabe Health Centre in Toronto and the Aboriginal Translators programs at the Civic Hospital in Regina, try to make health care accessible. However, there are few programs like the Toronto Street Patrol Program which tries to make life on the street survivable.

"We have volunteers go out in a van three to four times a week," explains Shirley Morrison. "We provide food, coffee, spare clothing and pass them out to the people on the street. Our volunteers are cops, doctors, social workers, people who know how to assess a situation and deal with it. We get a lot of co-operation from the police and from the city. Unfortunately, it's not funded by the provincial Ministry of Health. It all comes from the city and from what we can fund-raise ourselves."

Morrison knows the Street Patrol in Toronto isn't a solution to homelessness. "But we do go out and help people who would otherwise not get any help at all."

Housing

"Self-government for Aboriginal people is a dream that may come true," said Don Morin, the Northwest Territories Minister for Housing, recently to the Standing Committee of the House of Commons on Aboriginal Affairs. "We as Aboriginal people see this as a step in the right direction. However, when our people do not have a roof over their heads, the dream fades."

"When you have to pick up the body of a young adult who has blown his head off and you know this person had confided in you as to 'Why can't we get housing?', you know we must house our people – or self-government and all other dreams will become nightmares."

As Morin noted, along with unemployment, low income, limited education and addictions, housing remains a major problem with Aboriginal people wherever they live. Aboriginal people may migrate to urban areas in search of jobs and better housing, but they often end up unemployed and living in disappointing surroundings.

"The difficulties associated with obtaining and remaining satisfied with housing can be described within three major dimensions: access, adequacy, and quality," reported an Ontario Task Force on Urban Native Peoples in 1981. "As a general statement, it can be said that many Native people find it difficult to obtain housing, and those that do frequently complain about inadequate and poor quality conditions."

Native respondents' access to housing is limited by the objective shortage of housing, discrimination by landlords, limited finances, and information about housing availability. The shortages of housing are real and the consequences for people in all parts of the province are painful.

The study found housing shortages or poor quality housing were particular problems for Aboriginal elders, transients, people in crisis, and students. Older Aboriginal people may 'retire' to the cities because their reserves or communities lack the services they need. Aboriginal transients and people in crisis are often plagued by unemployment, high rents, discrimination and a lack of emergency shelters. The number of students living on minimal federal subsidies in urban centres in pursuit of an education has nearly tripled since 1981. "People are desperate for housing and will take almost anything no matter how high the rents," explained one of the respondents in the Ontario study.

Aboriginal people in urban centres are three times more likely to rent than to own their homes. They are more likely than non-Aboriginal people to live in crowded apartments and to face eviction. Their low income, lack of savings and lack of financial support, as well as the general lack of home-buying initiatives and low-income rental housing, contribute to the problems they face in the search for adequate housing in urban areas.

The Canada Mortgage and Housing Corporation (CMHC) has begun supporting Aboriginal housing programs in urban areas, but one Aboriginal administrator says, "there's one helluva need and we're not even getting close to filling it." Robin Henry says Kikinew Housing was established six years ago in Surrey, a Vancouver suburb. With the help of CMHC, Kikinew started with 44 units. Today it has 122 units and serves 500 families. It plans another 36 units in Chilliwack. Still, Henry says, "we're not keeping up."

"There's one family of 14 people living in a two-room unit. There are people living in motels, under bridges and in parks. It's a shame," adds June Latiear, the president of Kikinew Housing. "We have a priority list of clients, 25 per cent are needy, 25 per cent are on welfare, 25 per cent are elderly and 25 per cent are working."

Aside from some initial discrimination and opposition from neighbours and municipal officials, Henry says these programs can go a long way to provide adequate housing for some Aboriginal people in urban areas, "but not everyone". He says that while CMHC had some initial problems, "it's done a good job, cutting red tape, fast-tracking our proposals. It's just too bad they don't do that any more."

The municipal government in Surrey raised some initial objections and dragged its feet at first, Henry says. "It talked about crime, depressed land prices, kids running around." But Henry says the municipality has worked well with CMHC once the program started. However, he says, "there is no provincial program similar to CMHC that we can turn to. The province treats us just like any other program or group. We don't have priority. We have to compete with all of the other programs, and there just aren't enough units to go around."

The need for simple shelter, Henry says, is becoming critical. "I've got one lady who has three kids. Two of them sleep in the basement. There are rats down there. The kids covered the rat hole but I've got to get them into a decent place. But I've also got a husband who's abandoned his wife. She's sixteen and pregnant.

"I just don't have enough units."

Justice

Aboriginal people are swept up by every facet of the justice system in percentages far higher than their presence in the general population and much more than non-Aboriginal people. They are less likely to receive alternative sentencing, receive bail or get parole than non-Aboriginal Canadians. They are more likely to be incarcerated for a longer length of time than non-Aboriginal people.

According to the federal Solicitor General, Aboriginal people (Indian and Inuit) make up 10 per cent of the inmate population in federal penitentiaries, while they are only 2 per cent of the national population. They are far more likely to be involved with the justice system in western Canada than in eastern Canada. In some western provinces, where Aboriginal people make up about 10 per cent of the total population, the Aboriginal inmate population of federal penitentiaries is 40 per cent, while the Aboriginal population of provincial jails exceeds 50 per cent.

Aboriginal people are more likely to become involved with the justice system at a younger age than are non-Aboriginal people. They may first be apprehended by child welfare authorities, in much higher rates than non-Aboriginal people. This trend continues when they run afoul of the youth justice system, again at rates far higher than non-Aboriginal people. From these institutions, they 'graduate' into the adult justice system.

Many Aboriginal people are discriminated against by the justice system at every step. They feel discriminated against by the police, lawyers, Crown attorneys, judges and probation officers because of their differing cultures, societies and languages. They suffer because of their low social standing, low educational levels and high unemployment.

They are discriminated against because of their poverty, poor living conditions and the social problems in their communities. They lack normal protection for their rights because of the lack of involvement by their people in the justice system. They also suffer because justice officials, from police to judges, too often choose apprehension and punishment instead of discretion and alternatives to incarceration.

"Change will not come easily," advised the Commissioners of the Aboriginal Justice Inquiry in Manitoba. "But those in authority must commit themselves to massive reorganization and change. We believe that fundamental changes in philosophy, policy and programs are needed." The alternative, the Commissioners warned, was continued "frustration and bitterness" in Aboriginal communities.

As with other studies of the justice system and Aboriginal peoples such as the Donald Marshall, Jr., inquiry in Nova Scotia, the study into policing on the Blood Reserve in southern Alberta, and reviews in Saskatchewan and Ontario, the Manitoba inquiry recommended more hiring of Aboriginal people at all levels of the justice system; more cross-cultural training; more community-based programs; more job training for inmates; the use of alternatives to jail; more involvement by the Aboriginal community; more recognition of Aboriginal cultures and laws; and increased crime prevention.

It is also noted in every one of these studies, however, that there is very little attention paid to victim restitution or programs aimed at changing attitudes in Aboriginal communities toward crime. Most programs are aimed at handing out penalties to Aboriginal people after the crime has been committed.

Literacy

A few years ago, a survey conducted by the Southam News organization found that about five million people in Canada, or nearly one-fifth of the national population, couldn't read a newspaper, a manual or an advertisement. They were functionally illiterate.

Then, Statistics Canada had even more bad news. It estimated that about eight million Canadians, or about one-third of the population, was functionally illiterate. Many people could not read or write much more than their names.

These figures shocked people and governments at all levels. Many Canadians believed their system of education to be one of the best, most advanced and most accessible in the world. Yet the figures showed many people were undereducated and consigned to a life of poverty, dependency and ignorance. The social, economic and personal consequences were irrefutable and inescapable.

"Undereducated Canadians who are employed are mainly to be found in low-paying, potentially redundant jobs, with limited, if any, access to vocational training courses," reported the Royal Commission on Equality in Employment in 1984. "As individuals, they often lack the funds to undertake upgrading on their own. Yet without assistance they have little hope of improving their education level."

The situation for Aboriginal people was even worse. Some groups estimate that nearly one million Aboriginal people – between 40 and 65 per cent of the total Aboriginal population – are functionally illiterate, that is, between one-fifth and one-eighth of all the functionally illiterate people in Canada.

Depending on where Aboriginal people live, the drop-out rates before graduation from high school can be as high as 90 per cent. Many Aboriginal people have never gone beyond Grades 4 or 5. In 1981, the Royal Commission on Equality in Employment found that "42 per cent of the adult Native population had less than a Grade 9 education, twice the average for the Canadian population."

In reaction to the national literacy figures, the federal government announced the creation of the National Literacy Secretariat. The Secretariat "encourages partnership efforts in five key areas". It will fund groups to develop new learning materials; improve co-ordination and information sharing; increase public awareness; enhance access and outreach; and support "action research".

Aboriginal people find they don't benefit. The National Association of Friendship Centres (NAFC) conducted a survey of the Aboriginal literacy programs at its member centres and found that "It's an impossible task that isn't made easier by the confusing, and often conflicting, policies of the funding agencies. While Aboriginal people are a federal responsibility, it says Native literacy programs fall under provincial jurisdiction. And neither level of government funds local Aboriginal language projects. The result is a hodge-podge of funding programs, differing from province to province.

The National Literacy Secretariat transfers millions of dollars to the provinces and territories to cover up to 50 per cent of the cost of literacy initiatives. But little of this money trickles down to help Aboriginal literacy projects.

The NAFC survey also identified a "vague" definition of literacy that excludes Aboriginal people from literacy programs because they don't have enough education – literacy programs are aimed primarily at "upgrading the skills" of the functionally illiterate with Grade 8 education and above. It cited a lack of day-care facilities and other forms of support for learners, in particular unemployed, single parents.

Migratory Patterns

> Andrea is a 20-year old Inuit woman from Cape Dorset in the Northwest Territories. Her mother died when she was 14 years old. Andrea has four sisters and brothers. Shortly after the death of her mother, Andrea's father remarried, to a woman with seven children of her own. Andrea was unable to get along with her siblings and step-mother.
>
> Andrea first came to Montreal with the aid of Health and Welfare Canada for treatment of a hearing problem. At this time, she began hanging out in bars frequented by other Inuit. Andrea missed two flights home and finally had to pay for her own flight back to Cape Dorset. After she returned home, she decided to leave and return to Montreal. Andrea has been on the streets of Montreal for the last three years.
>
> Case Study # 2
> Needs Assessment Study
> Native Friendship Centre of Montreal (1986)

Sometime after the Second World War, Aboriginal people began what some people call the "First Wave" into urban centres. This first, large migratory movement of Aboriginal people from reserves and settlements peaked in the mid-1960s.

An Aboriginal baby boom in the 1960s combined with several other factors to provoke this migration. The most important were severe economic conditions, poor housing, inadequate resources, limited educational opportunities, and high rates of unemployment and alcohol abuse in their home communities. There's also no doubt that many of these Aboriginal migrants were seeking jobs, an education, better housing and adequate social services.

Some Aboriginal people continue to move, returning back and forth between urban centres and their home communities. However, many Aboriginal people remain in urban centres. They are far more likely to rent homes, to change addresses more often and to live in poorer neighbourhoods than non-Aboriginal people. They are also more likely to migrate between urban centres and other regions of the country than non-Aboriginal Canadians.

It is difficult to obtain reliable statistics. The population figures provided by the Department of Indian Affairs, provincial agencies and Aboriginal organizations are not always accurate. The Manitoba Aboriginal Justice Inquiry, for instance, found that "problems exist with the assumptions on which the reports of each of these agencies are based." It hired a private firm to compile statistics to determine Manitoba's total Aboriginal population (Indian, Inuit and Métis).

This firm, Dansys Consultants, estimated that Manitoba's Aboriginal population in 1991 was 130,000, representing more than 11 per cent of the provincial population. The Department of Indian Affairs and Northern Development does not include Métis, and its estimates show that Aboriginal people make up about five per cent of the Manitoba population. Dansys estimated that 33 per cent of Manitoba's Aboriginal population, or 41,000 people, live in the city of Winnipeg, where they make up about 6.5 per cent of the city's total population.

Recent figures for the Aboriginal population of Toronto and Edmonton show similar differences of opinion. Government estimates suggest there are 33, 000 Aboriginal people living in the city of Toronto, while Aboriginal organizations double the estimate to 80,000. The 1982 Census puts the Aboriginal population of Edmonton at about 12,000, while Aboriginal leaders estimate that the figure today is closer to 50,000.

Whatever figures one chooses to rely upon, it is obvious that Aboriginal people are continuing to migrate to urban centres. From studies in Ontario, Manitoba and Saskatchewan, we know they are moving for many of the same reasons. We also know they are encountering many of the same problems their predecessors faced in the 1960s.

They continue to move for jobs, better housing, education, training, social services and the hope of a better future. However, they also continue to face a lack of or inadequate housing, discrimination, unemployment and cultural alienation. A study of urban Aboriginal people in Ontario found they still confront "a frustrating gap between hope and reality, limited funds, exasperating experiences with urban institutions and inexperience with big city life."

Poverty

> Indian families are more likely to be single-parent families, especially off-reserve, where 36 per cent are single parent families, compared to the provincial and reserve average, both at 18 per cent.
>
> Manitoba Public Inquiry into the
> Administration of Justice and Aboriginal People
> (Aboriginal Justice Inquiry)

It is no secret that Aboriginal people have been and continue to be on the bottom rung of the economic ladder in Canada. Economic conditions on Indian reserves and Métis settlements have been described as "severely depressed". Many Aboriginal people, particularly Aboriginal men, gravitate to the cities in search of an education or jobs. Aboriginal women are more likely to be following family members or escaping "problems on the reserve or home communities."

However, they are often unable to find work. They then face unemployment, poverty, inadequate housing and poor health care. For many Aboriginal people, the promise of a better life in the cities is only an illusion.

The economic situation for Aboriginal peoples has deteriorated over the past ten years. Between 1981 and 1986, although more Aboriginal people were entering the work force, there were also more Aboriginal people earning less than their non-Aboriginal counterparts, more joining the ranks of the unemployed, more depending on welfare, more homeless, and more experiencing extreme poverty. There is every reason to believe the situation has worsened since 1986, given the general downturn in the economy.

Hardest hit were single-parent and large families. According to one study, "more than 81 per cent of Regina's native households received incomes below the poverty line. The incidence of poverty is only slightly lower among Saskatoon's Native population. Although poverty affects a significant portion of households of all types in both cities, single-parent families in particular are most likely to experience problems in income adequacy. Less than 10 per cent of these households received incomes above the poverty line."

The Aboriginal Justice Inquiry (AJI) found similar economic conditions in Manitoba. Aboriginal people in Manitoba had an average income that was one-third less than that of non-Aboriginal people in the rest of the province. There were twice as many Aboriginal people reporting no incomes at all compared to non-Aboriginal people in Manitoba. Similar comparisons exist across Canada.

The AJI also found 'official' unemployment rates vastly underestimate actual unemployment rates when it took into account people who had stopped registering for work with Employment and Immigration Canada because "there are simply no jobs to be had".

"The unemployment rate for Manitoba's Indian population is 26.3 per cent, compared to 7.6 per cent for the total provincial population," the Commissioners wrote. "We believe that the actual rate of unemployment among Aboriginal people in some communities is two to three times higher than that."

A study conducted by the Winnipeg Social Planning Council found that "more than one-half of the Aboriginal households exist below the poverty line, compared to about 20 per cent of non-Aboriginal households."

Women are particularly hard hit. In a study conducted by the Native Friendship Centre of Montreal (NFCM) in 1986, researchers looked at the lives of 39 homeless or marginalized women. The study found the situation of these particular women was much more common than previously realized. The study found that Aboriginal women "are the least educated, possess the least number of marketable skills, have difficulties with the working languages of Quebec, [and have] little or no contact with social service agencies of any type." Adding to their difficulties were "cultural differences which are negatively perceived by the larger society."

The NFCM study states that, for these reasons, "legitimate, permanent and gainful employment is almost a virtual impossibility" for a number of Aboriginal women in urban centres like Montreal. Nearly one-quarter of the Aboriginal women surveyed described themselves as "professional prostitutes". The majority of the 39 women studied were described by the authors as "survival prostitutes" who solicited "in order to meet their basic needs – shelter, food, clothing, cigarettes, alcohol and drugs... They solicit in order to survive."

Of the 39 Aboriginal women surveyed, one-third were functionally illiterate. Fewer than half the women had completed high school. They lacked skills and training to find and keep jobs. Three-quarters were welfare recipients. "In Quebec," the NFCM concluded, "welfare payments...are insufficient to meet even basic needs. Of necessity...given their limited access to the job market...it is not surprising that many of these women turn to illegal activities in order to survive."

Many studies have concluded that the poverty of Aboriginal people in urban areas is compounded by an unwillingness of the three levels of government (federal, provincial and municipal) to take responsibility. Aboriginal people "fall between the cracks of government programs" when they arrive in the cities.

When Indians leave the reserve, the federal government relinquishes its obligations to them. They lose the right to free or subsidized housing (often provided by the band), social programs, exemption from income tax and other payroll benefits, exemption from property taxes, and (outside Alberta) exemption from provincial sales taxes for goods used on-reserve. The provincial government does not recognize any special rights for Indians. When Natives come to Edmonton to escape the hardships of their communities, their benefits are taken away.

Appendices
Round Table Program

21-23 June 1992
Edmonton, Alberta

Sunday, 21 June 1992

7:00 p.m.- 9:00 p.m.
Registration/Reception

> *Welcoming Remarks by Deputy Mayor of Edmonton, Sheila McKay*
>
> *Welcoming Remarks by Commission Co-Chairs*
>
> *Introductions:*
> Elder Joe Cardinal
> Commissioners
> Executive Director
> Commission Secretary
> Directors
> Co-Facilitators
> Round Table Facilitators

Monday, 22 June 1992

7:30 a.m.
Registration

8:30 a.m.
Opening Prayer
> Elder Joe Cardinal

8:45 a.m.
Opening Remarks and Overview of Round Table
> Dianne Moir and Michael Thrasher, Co-Facilitators

9:00 a.m.
Background Presentation
> Dr. Lloyd Barber

10:00 a.m.
Problem and Obstacle Identification Workshops
    Services
    Economics
    Health
    Governance

12:00 p.m.
Lunch

1:30 p.m.
Panel Discussions: Successful Models
    (Panelists subject to change)

    Services
    Panelists:
    Teresa Stevenson, Chili for Children, Regina

    Katherine Morriseau-Sinclair, Co-founder,
    Abinochi Zhawayndakozihwin Ojibway Language Program, Winnipeg

    Connie Campbell, Regional Director,
    Metis Child and Family Services, Edmonton

    Clifford Summers, Executive Director,
    Aboriginal Legal Services, Toronto

    Economics
    Panelists:
    Roy Cunningham, Chair,
    Aboriginal Opportunities Committee of Calgary Chamber of Commerce,
    Calgary

    Lois Frank, Chair,
    Treaty Seven Business Development Centre, Calgary

    Linda Clarkson, Writer, Policy Adviser, Winnipeg

    Patrick Lavelle, President, Canadian Council for Native Business, Toronto

    Governance
    Panelists:
    Eugene Arcand, Vice-Chief,
    Federation of Saskatchewan Indian Nations, Saskatchewan

    Rodney Bobiwash, Urban Native Self-Government Co-ordinator,
    Native Canadian Centre of Toronto

    Eric Robinson, President,
    Winnipeg First Nations Council, Winnipeg

Grace Appleyard, President,
Metis Women of Manitoba

Health

Panelists:
Leonard Johnston,
Healing Our Spirit, AIDS Society, Vancouver

Maggie Hodgson, Executive Director,
Nechi Institute, Edmonton

Ida Labillois-Williams, Executive Director,
Native Friendship Centre of Montreal

3:45 p.m.
Generating Alternatives Workshops

Services

Economics

Health

Governance

6:00 p.m.
Closing Prayer
Elder Joe Cardinal

Tuesday, 23 June 1992

8:30 a.m.
Opening Prayer
Elder Joe Cardinal

8:40 a.m.
Plenary Session
Facilitator to refocus on Round Table objectives

9:00 a.m.
Strategies for Implementation Workshops

Services

Economics

Health

Governance

11:30 a.m.
Lunch

1:00 p.m.
Community-Specific Strategies for Implementation Workshops

Winnipeg

Edmonton

Vancouver

Montreal

Toronto

Saskatoon

Halifax

Regina

Calgary

3:00 p.m.
Plenary Panel on Community-Specific Strategies

4:00 p.m.
Co-Chairs/Commissioners' Discussion on Policy and Community-Specific Strategies

5:00 p.m.
Closing Prayer
Elder Joe Cardinal

Round Table Participants

Alderman Fritz
Alderman Schmal
Albert, Bernice
Anctel, Jason
Anderson, Linda
Angnatuk, Elijah
Appleyard, Grace
Arcand, Sylvia
Arcand, Lorna
Arcand, Eugene
Ashawasega, Augustin
Ashley, K. Michael
Atleo, Clifford Sr.
Bailey, Dickson
Baldwin, William Archie
Barber, Lloyd Dr.
Barron, Dave
Bastien, Betty
Beach, Debra
Bear, Lori
Beaudoin, Kim
Beaver, Alfred
Belcourt, Gordon
Belcourt, Jodi-Lynn
Belhumer, Terry
Bergeron, Chris
Berlin, Mark
Bernhardt, Wilma
Bird, Ernest

Bitternose, Ron
Boadway, Robin
Bobiwash, A. Rodney
Boudria, James
Bouvier, Ephram
Bragg, Cathy
Budesheim, Barb
Burns, Dennis
Campbell, Connie
Campbell, Teresa
Canada, Deborah
Cardinal, Perez
Carlson, Nellie
Carr, Cheryl Ann
Castel, Ronald
Champagne, Robert
Charlie, Barbara
Chartier, Mrs. S.
Chartrand, David
Chartrand, Florence
Chaske, Ivy
Chaske, Richard
Choinieré, J.G.
Clairmont, Lynda
Clairmount, Linda
Clark, Nancy
Clarkson, Linda
Cloutier, Edith
Coates, Ken

Coffin, Edma
Colley, Vern E.
Connell, Glenn
Cooper, Deborah
Cooper, Holly
Corrigan, Chris
Crawford, George
Croft, Minnie
Cunningham, Roy
D'Aubin, April
Davidee, Ida
Davis, Mike
Dejardin, Ray
Dejardin, Melanie
Delaronde, Dina
Demas, Doreen
Demerais, Lou
Desmeules, Ann
DeWolfe, Greg
Dickason, Olive
Dorey, Dwight
Doxtator, Terry
Dubois, Roland
Duchesne, J.
Esquimaux-Hamlin,
    R. Jackie
Ferguson, Holly
Fiala, Jackie
Fisher, Georgina

Fletcher, John
Fonatine, Carol
Fontaine-Brighstar,
    Marilyn
Fossneuve, Roy
Fayant, Jason
Francois, Tom
Frank, Lois
Fraser, Irene
Fraser, Allyson
Friedel, Marge
Fulham, Richard
Gaudet, Marie
Gerlock, Amy
Gervais, Laverne
Giesbrecht, Winnie
Gilroy, Ernie
Giovanatti, Marie
Gladue, Helen
Glover, Dorothea
Goetz, Ralph
Gryba, Mark
Haineault, Bill
Hall, Darlene
Hamilton, Murray
Harper, Louis
Harper, Pat
Helgason, Wayne
Henderson, May
Hill, Josie
Hodgson, Maggie
Hopkins, Betty
Houle, Nora
Hourie, Audreen
House, Theresa
Hull, Wendy
Inkster, George
Ironstar, Sharon
Jacko, Adelard
Jackson, Gillan
Janvier, Wally

Johnston, Leonard
Kakaway, Walter
Kelley, Annie
King, Gordon
King, Cecil
Kirkness, Andrew
Kramble, Bryan
Kraushaar, Brigitte
L'Hirondelle, Andre
Lajambe, Deanna
Lancelay, Darlene
Langlois, Pierre
Laurin, Nova
Lavalle, Jules
Lavelle, Patrick
Lefort, Lana
Letendre, Bruce
Liles, David
Liskowich, Candace
Littlechief, Roy
Loeuen, Jeff
Long, Richard
Lyle, Donald
MacGregor, Lorrie
MacKenzie, Wayne
Magnuson, Earl
Mallett, George H.
Mandamin, Tony
Manningway, Solomon
Maple, Damon
Marchuk, Russell
Martel, Lloyd
Martial, Rose
Martin, David Joseph
Mason, Gayle
McCormick, Marileen
McKay, Winston
McLeod, Lucille
McLeod, Albert
McMaster, Laverna
McNally, D.D.

McQuabbie, Robert
McTaggart, Malcolm J.
Meadmore, Marion
    Ironquil
Moisiuk, Sherri
Montague, Murray
Monture-Malloch,
    Barbara
Morin, Donna
Morriseau-Sinclair,
    Katherine
Nofield, Edward
Norris, F.D.
Obed, Joseph
Ortiz, Theresa
Panegyuk, David Papak
Parenteau, Lillian
Paris, Danielle
Parsons, Sandra
Paul, Arthur G.
Pefin, Mabel
Pelletier, Tina
Perron, Maurice
Peters, Pat
Pettifer, Carolyn
Pilquil, Carlos
Plante, Stan
Pleasant-Jette, Corine
    Mont
Poisson, René
Pranteau, David
Pratt, Anita
Prefontaine, Daniel
Quinney, Norman
Rabesca, Bertha
Racette, Dona
Ragush, Don
Raven, James
Redwood, Lawrence
Reynolds, Tony
Rider, Keith

Rivard, Ron
Robinson, Eric
Ronnenberg, Doris
Ross, Clair
Roy, Tom J.
Russell, Peter H.
Samuel, Wally
Sanderson, Nelson
Seneca, Brad
Sims, Valerie
Sinclair, Paul M.
Slattery, Brian
Slauenwhite, Darilea
Slippery, Darwin
Smith, Michel
Smith, Isabelle
Sonnichsen, Paul
Sorbey, Katherine
Soucie, Debra
Sparrow, Gail
St. Arneault, Delilah
Staniscia, Mary
Stefanson, Kris,
    Chief Judge
Sterling, Doreen
Stevenson, Theresa
Stevenson, Greg
Still, Daniel
Summers, Clifford
Sutton, Lloyd
Taylor, Victor
Teneese, Kathryn
Terriak, Robert
Thatcher, Francis
Thusky, Veronique
Ulrich, Gary
Wagner, Eric
Webster, Larry
Welsh, Robert
White, Marjorie
Williams, Ida

Willier, Mary
Wilson, Don
Wilson-Kenny, Dara
Wood-Steiman, Pauline
Wortman, Jay
Yauk, Tom
Young, Thomas W.
Zander, Bonnie
Zoe, John B.

Elder:
Joe Cardinal

Commission Staff:
Jean T. Fournier
Jerome Berthelette
John Morrisseau
David Hawkes
Marlene Brant-
    Castellano
Kim Scott
Karen Collins
Kathryn Boissoneau
Charlene Wysote
Katherine Livingstone
Allen Gabriel
Don Kelly

**Round Table
Facilitators:**
Diane Moir
Michael Thrasher
Rob Foss
Roy Chambers
Muriel Stanley-Venne
George Calliou
Jane Sager
Laurent Roy
Clayton Blook
Chester Cunningham
Carola Cunningham